A CENTURY AT THE BAR
OF THE SUPREME COURT OF
THE UNITED STATES

A Century at the Bar
of the Supreme Court of
the United States

By CHARLES HENRY BUTLER

Former Reporter of Decisions
of the Court

ILLUSTRATED

G · P · PUTNAM'S SONS · *New York*

To

CHARLES EVANS HUGHES

ELEVENTH CHIEF JUSTICE OF THE

UNITED STATES

THIS BOOK IS DEDICATED

WITH THE HIGHEST ESTEEM

AND DEEPEST AFFECTION

OF THE AUTHOR

FOREWORD

O N FEBRUARY 1, 1940 in the City of Washington exercises were held to commemorate the sesquicentennial of the founding of the Supreme Court. At that time my father, Charles Henry Butler, who had been a member of the Bar of that Court for over half a century, had all but finished the manuscript of A CENTURY AT THE BAR OF THE SUPREME COURT OF THE UNITED STATES. He had told Chief Justice Charles Evans Hughes of his desire to dedicate this book to him and had received his consent. There remained some names and dates to be verified, some incidents and stories to be corroborated and the chapter describing the centennial and the sesquicentennial activities to be completed in the light of events which were at that moment taking place.

The day following the sesquicentennial activities, in which the author formally took part, he became ill, and on February 9, 1940 he died without having completed the manuscript.

The finishing touches would have been comparatively simple for the author, who had in mind which names and dates required verification, which incidents corroboration and where to find the information. For others to complete that task since his death has required far more time and research. Hence, this book, which the author had expected to publish on June 18, 1940, his eighty-first birthday, is only now in print.

It is my privilege to arrange for the publication of this

book. If it reminds those who knew the author of his dynamic personality, if it affords interest to others, and especially if it instills in those who read it the same respect and devotion which the author always had for the Supreme Court of the United States, its members and the high traditions for which it has always stood, its publication will be amply justified.

HENRY F. BUTLER

Washington, D.C.
December, 1941

INTRODUCTORY AND ALSO APOLOGETIC, EXPLANATORY AND VINDICATORY

AN INTRODUCTION is supposed to give the reader some idea, or at least some intimation, of what may be expected in the book about to be perused. There may also be an implied obligation to fulfil the reader's expectations in this respect, and to explain the why, wherefore and the direction of the author's firing his broadside. Thus innocent bystanders are enabled to escape before the firing, or, as in this case, the reading begins.

Writing of various forms of introductory addresses to which he had been subjected during a lecture tour, Irvin Cobb described as the least objectionable, one delivered by a man who stood up on the platform and said:

"My friends, I've been told that if I'd introduce Mr. Cobb he'd make a speech. I've done it. He'll do it."

Many friends have told me that if these reminiscences were published, they would read them. Paraphrasing the foregoing:

"Now I've published 'em. You read 'em."

Nearly every autobiography begins with an apology by the author for inflicting an account of his personal experiences on his readers and ending with a hope for their indulgence. In the bottom of his heart, however, he cherishes the idea that he is rendering the world a great service in preserving for all time a record of what has happened to himself, and also that he is affording instruction and enjoyment to a vast army of readers, whose members will put his book at the top of the list of non-fiction best-sellers.

These expectations are usually doomed to be shattered—

as mine would be if any such existed—when, on entering one of our modern drug stores, in which everything is sold except drugs, he beholds many copies of his *magnum opus* on the Nineteen-Cent Counter on which "publishers' surplus stocks" are being offered. In contemplation he may recall the lines of Gray's immortal "Elegy":

> Full many a gem of purest ray serene
> The dark, unfathomed caves of ocean bear;
> Full many a flower is born to blush unseen,
> And waste its sweetness on the desert air.

The author may console himself, however, by attributing his non-success to the inability of the public to appreciate his work. A playwright once explained to me that his latest play had been, in the parlance of the theater, a "flop" because theatergoers were simply "too dumb" to comprehend what he was trying to tell them. "In fact," he added, "I've been casting my pearls before swine."

So much for the apologetic part of this introduction. Now for its explanatory and vindicatory elements. *Vindicatory* should not be confused with *vindictive*. Webster clearly differentiates the two words. He uses *justificatory* as a synonym of *vindicatory*. It is my hope that the reader, after finishing this volume, will feel the author has been vindicated, or at least has been justified in yielding to the pleas of over-zealous friends for its publication. In that event the verdict might be either, "guilty with recommendation for mercy," or else, "not guilty, but don't do it again."

As to the explanatory element, it is, perhaps, easier to explain what the book is not, rather than what it is. It is not an autobiography, although necessarily it contains references to events happening during the author's life and in which he participated. It is not several biographies rolled into one. It is not a family history. Nor is it a history of the Supreme Court of the United States, although that body is frequently referred to.

There are many such histories. Among the most notable

are two: that of Hampton L. Carson, which covers the first century of the Court's existence, and that of Charles Warren, which covers a longer period. Both these histories are not only of high literary and high legal merit, but also they are exceedingly interesting reading for laymen as well as for lawyers. The Judiciary Committee of the United States Senate should, in my opinion, make it a *sine qua non* that a nominee for a judicial office should have studied these volumes before his nomination could be voted on favorably.

To those interested in statistics and details is recommended a small but interesting book entitled "The Judges of the Supreme Court 1789-1937" published by Professor Corteaz A. M. Ewing of the University of Oklahoma. It contains a great deal of valuable information compressed into its 124 pages.

This effort of mine, it should be said furthermore, is not a digest of the Court's opinions, which may be found in more than 300 volumes of the Court's Reports. Fifty-five of these volumes were issued during my Reportership. All the opinions are readily accessible. Not all of them perhaps are understandable to laymen and some of them possibly not even to lawyers.

Regarding further explanation, let me follow the example set by the eminent sculptor of a famous statue in a Washington cemetery. In answer to questioners who asked what the remarkable image meant, he would say: "Have you seen it?" On receiving an affirmative reply he would add: "Then you know what it means."

So to any reader inquiring what this is all about, my reply is that whatever the reactions of that reader may be, that is exactly what it is about. Also it is my hope that my readers may have as much pleasure in the perusal of these pages as has been mine in writing them.

It is my sincere wish, moreover, that whatever other reactions may result from the reading of these reminiscences it will be realized that as far as possible it has been my endeavor, in depicting the relations of my family to the Supreme Court of the United States, to accentuate the reverence and respect every member of it has always had for that high tribunal and for those who have sat upon its bench. A further aim has been to show, in the sketches of my grandfather and of my father, not only the high legal ability that gained for them the respect of their associates at the Bar and of the judges before whom they practiced, but also the nobility of character they both possessed and which endeared them to their home communities.

William Allen Butler, my father, begins the introduction to his "Retrospect of Forty Years"—on the seventy-fourth anniversary of his birth, February 20, 1899—by saying:

". . . being by the blessing of Providence of 'sound mind and memory' . . . 'and under no restraint' save a somewhat impaired eyesight, it seems to me an opportune moment for beginning a narrative of some of the events of a long and busy life.

"I am moved to this more by calls, urgent and reiterated, from the voices of those nearest and dearest to me, than by any decided impulse of my own." *

He continues:

"I believe it is Henri Rochefort, the Parisian journalist, who is credited with the cynical remark that when men become fit for nothing else they begin to write their reminiscences. This is an apt illustration of the old legal maxim: 'The greater the truth, the greater the libel' . . . for it is only when they are disabled for the active pursuits of life that they can find solace and refuge in memory.

"It is often said that old men live in the past; but would it not be truer to say that the past lives in them, so far as they revive its recollections and chronicle its events? Surely they ought not to be grudged this harmless monopoly of reminiscences."

Perhaps it was as a warning to others—including probably myself—that he added to the foregoing:

"Fortunately, perhaps, a safeguard against too much autobiography is found in the fact that so many personal memoirs,

* The italics are mine.—C.H.B.

begun with good intent, are never carried to completion. . . . In a sense what the Bible is to the race, the record of every man's life is to himself, a revelation in which he may read the designs and dealings of Providence, his own human lapses and the divine deliverances.

"The interest we take in our own lives is incommunicable. Only as they have been linked with other lives more potential than our own, can they have any special interest even to our kindred."

This idea of my father's is almost identical with that expressed by my friend, the eminent and interesting journalist, Mark Sullivan, who, in a conversation about the possibility of my publishing some reminiscences to be based largely on entries in the Guest Book of our Washington home, said:

"Nobody cares whether So-and-so, no matter how distinguished, did or did not dine with *you;* but if that distinguished person, while dining with you, *did* or *said* something worth recording, then everybody would be interested in what that person did or said."

This is very true, although somewhat shattering to an author's estimate of his own personality.

Much might be said about the tendency of one who has reached my years of indiscretion to recount to his friends events which happened years ago and in which he participated. If his listeners are polite, the narrator, sometimes pathetically in error, thinks they are also really interested. Regarding this propensity—which, let us hope, in the present case will be controlled if not overcome—there is a story: After having listened patiently to the recollections of their host while enjoying his very good dinner, one of the guests said to another as they walked home together:

"Poor old N——! His dinner was splendid, but his stories—it really seems as though he's in his dotage."

"Oh, no, indeed," returned the other; "he's only in his *anecdotage.*"

The Messengers of the Supreme Court of the United States, a band of the most faithful and painstaking public servants that ever lived, have many opportunities to tell of happenings of which they know because of their intimate relations with the Justices in the performance of their duties. Not one of them, however, has ever been known to betray his trust by disclosing anything within his knowledge.

For many years the dean of the Messenger corps was Archie Lewis. He was appointed by Chief Justice Roger Brooke Taney, and faithfully served the Court for nearly sixty-four years until his death in 1913. During his last years his sole duties were in the Robing Room, looking after the Justices' gowns and adjusting them on the wearers before they went into the courtroom. One day someone suggested to Archie that he write his reminiscences. Archie asked to be told what "reminiscences" were. It was explained to him that as he had been in the Robing Room for so many years with the Justices, he must know a lot of stories about them that would make interesting reading.

To this Archie is said to have replied that the Justices had come and gone so fast he could not keep track of them, and, besides, he had always been so busy taking care of the robes and seeing that the Justices put them on right before going on the bench, he had no time to write stories, even if he would, about what went on in the Robing Room.

Yet how much more interesting Archie's reminiscences might have been than any my pen and memory can produce!

Having advanced good and sufficient reason why the production and circulation of my reminiscences should be forever forbidden and enjoined, it now behooves me to plead that sentence to that effect should be suspended. It should be suspended, at least, with regard to the earlier sections, on the ground that they do not relate exclusively to myself. Chiefly they concern various and much more interesting incidents in the lives of other members of my family, during their continuous membership at the Bar of the Supreme Court of the United States since 1832.

There is an oft-told, but perhaps applicable, story about

a lawyer who had so thoroughly prepared himself by study-
ing all precedents for and against his client that in his opening argument he presented his opponent's case so strongly
his client pulled his coat-tails and whispered:

"You are arguing this case against me."

"Keep still," retorted his lawyer.

Yet, realizing he had been doing that very thing, the
lawyer continued his address as follows:

"Now, Your Honor, these are the insidious arguments that
will be presented by my learned opponent, but which, it will
be conclusively demonstrated, are wholly inapplicable in this
case and are without foundation in law or in fact."

The lawyer then proceeded with his argument to the sat-
isfaction of his client, not only as to his presentation of the
case, but also as to the decision subsequently rendered in his
favor.

The actual moving cause for my father's writing his "Retrospect of Forty Years," as quoted in his own words, is applicable in my own case. It may be even more so, perhaps,
because at eighty—six years older than he was when he wrote
—those urgent and reiterated calls from the same kind voices
have come to me from a longer period than his. When the
respondent reaches the Psalmist's three score years and ten,
his nearest and dearest grow anxious for the beginning as
well as the completion of the task of transforming oral traditions into what may become permanent history.

Benjamin Franklin Butler, my grandfather, became a
member of the Bar of the Supreme Court of the United
States on March 5, 1832. Since that date members of his
family, sixteen in all, and always one at least bearing the
name Butler, have continually been members of that Bar.
In the year 1940 his line was represented by one grandson,
one grandson-in-law, and five great grandsons.

Less than two years after his admission, Benjamin F.
Butler became Attorney General of the United States. This
office he held from 1833 to 1838, in the administration of

President Andrew Jackson and that of President Martin Van Buren. Twice thereafter he served as United States Attorney for the Southern District of New York.

My father, William Allen Butler, was admitted to the Bar of the Court, on the motion of Attorney General Reverdy Johnson, on April 4, 1850.

My own admission to the Bar was on the motion of Joseph H. Choate, on March 16, 1886.

My brother, William Allen Butler, Jr. and my son, Henry F. Butler, were both admitted on my motion; the former on January 3, 1910, and the latter on November 13, 1933.

Soon after my admission, it was my privilege to serve on a committee of the Bar Association of New York of which William M. Evarts was chairman, and which did effective work in persuading Congress to increase the inadequate salaries of the Justices of the Supreme Court. At the celebration in 1890 of the one hundredth anniversary of the first session of the Court, it was my lot, as one of the members of the Judiciary Centennial Committee, also to be on the subcommittee in charge of the banquet, which was one of the principal features of the occasion.

The activities told of here have concerned the Court as a unit, but the relations of my family with the members of the Court have been delightfully pleasant from a purely personal standpoint, from the time my grandfather first appeared before it.

During my clerkship in my father's office, from 1879 to 1884, the period of my legal education, which was not obtained from any college or law school, often my father asked me to accompany him to Washington when he was to appear before the Court to argue a case. It was my good fortune on these occasions not only to see all the members of the Court as they listened to him as an advocate, but also frequently to meet some of them in friendly interviews either in the court room, or, later in the day, at their homes, where Father was always a welcome guest.

My Reportership in the Supreme Court of the United States began in December, 1902, and put me in close personal and friendly social contact with the Chief Justice and the Associate Justices, until my retirement in 1916. Thereafter that association was not so close, yet the same friendly relations have continued ever since, not only with those who united in their signed farewell tribue to me, but also with their successors.

The elementary legal and ethical principles that no man should be the judge in his own case, and that one who is his own lawyer has a fool for a client, are as familiar to me as they are to every other member of the Bar. Nor can one be unmindful of the admonitions of the Supreme Court of the United States, which are equally applicable to individuals and to commissions charged with regulating industrial, civic and personal activities, that no one can act in the same proceeding as grand jury, prosecuting attorney, judge and trial jury, and determine every issue involved and penalize an offender accordingly.

Notwithstanding all this, and functioning in all the above-mentioned capacities—including that of the client acting as his own lawyer—my determination is—as they say in law and sometimes in politics—"to go to the country," and publish these reminiscences. The final decision as to the wisdom and success of such action is left to the one infallible and uncontrollable court, public opinion. Even if it does not approve of my decision, I hope that it will not condemn me too severely for deciding the case in my own favor, entering judgment, putting the same into execution and taking such proceedings thereunder as are in accord with the decision so made.

More than one person has told the author that the title of this book is misleading, because it conveys the idea that he himself has been a member of the Bar of the Supreme Court of the United States for at least one hundred years.

His reply has been that while such is not the case, his grandfather, his father, his son and he himself have been continually members of the Bar of that Court for more than a century, and that the title relates to these members of his family.

The author does not claim that his family is the only one that has had continuous membership at the Bar of the Supreme Court of the United States for a century or more, but he does not know of any other family with so large a membership and with continuous representation of the same name for so long a period.

As this book has been written for lay as well as for legal readers, authorities for statements have not been included in the text. Except when expressly disclaimed, every statement is supported by an authority, whether cited or not.

During the time of preparation of this volume for publication, which period has lasted several years, there have been five changes in the personnel of the Supreme Court. These were due to the retirement of Messrs. Justices Van Devanter, Sutherland and Brandeis, and to the death of Messrs. Justices Cardozo and Butler. They were replaced in like order by Messrs. Justices Black, Reed, Frankfurter, Douglas and Murphy. This has been a period of one of the most rapid changes in the history of the Court.

This preface cannot be concluded without an expression of gratitude to Mr. Cropley, the Clerk of the Court, Mr. Waggaman, the Marshal, Mr. Knaebel, the Reporter of Decisions, Mr. Vance and Mr. Clark, the Law Librarians, and to the members of their respective staffs—not, however, making them *particeps criminis*—for kindness and consideration shown during many years. Without their aid and assistance it would have been impossible for these reminiscences to have been completed as it would have been difficult for the Court itself to function in administering not only the law but that unfailing justice of which it is the country's faithful guardian.

CONTENTS

CONTENTS

ILLUSTRATIONS

xxi

ILLUSTRATIONS

A CENTURY AT THE BAR
OF THE SUPREME COURT OF
THE UNITED STATES

CHAPTER I

MY GRANDFATHER AND HIS RELATIONS WITH THE SUPREME COURT OF THE UNITED STATES

MY GRANDFATHER, Benjamin F. Butler, of Albany, New York, was admitted to the Bar of the Supreme Court of the United States in his thirty-seventh year, on motion of William Wirt, March 5th, 1832. Mr. Wirt had been Attorney General of the United States from 1817 to 1829, the longest period of tenure of that office before or since.

Andrew Jackson was then President of the United States. Roger B. Taney, his first Attorney General, had been transferred to the office of Secretary of the Treasury, but his appointment was not confirmed by the Senate. Those were the hectic days of the political battles regarding the United States Bank, its charter and Government deposits.

On the death of Chief Justice John Marshall in 1835, Taney was appointed by the President to succeed that great jurist and, after a long struggle with the Senate, his appointment was confirmed. Meanwhile the President selected my grandfather to fill the vacancy resultant from the transfer of Taney from the Attorney Generalship. My Grandfather's commission was dated November 15th, 1833. One hundred years less two days thereafter, my son Henry Franklin Butler, whose middle name was in memory of his great grandfather, was admitted to the Bar of the Supreme Court on his thirty-seventh birthday. Thus Henry Franklin Butler continued the second century of the family's membership in the Supreme Court Bar at almost the same age

1

SUPREME COURT OF THE UNITED STATES OF AMERICA.

I, WILLIAM THOMAS CARROLL, *Clerk of the Supreme Court of the United States,*
Do hereby certify, That B. F. Butler Esquire
of the State of New York
was duly admitted and qualified, as an Attorney and Counsellor of the said Supreme
Court of the United States, on the Fifth *day of*
March *in the year of our Lord one thousand eight hundred*
and thirty two *and of the Independence of the United States*
of America, the Fifty Sixth *.*

IN TESTIMONY WHEREOF, *I have hereunto*
set my hand and affixed the Seal of the said
Supreme Court, at the City of Washington,
this Fifth *day of*
March *in the year of our Lord*
one thousand eight hundred and thirty two*.*

Wm. Th. Carroll
Clk. Sup. Ct. U. S.

as that at which his progenitor became Attorney General
of the United States.

William Wirt, a close friend of my grandfather, was one
of the most eminent lawyers of his day and well known
throughout the country during his legal and political career.
He died on the morning of February 18, 1834. On receipt
of the news the Supreme Court adjourned on motion of my

grandfather, who immediately thereafter presided at a meeting of the Bar of the Supreme Court. Resolutions of sorrow and respect were prepared by Daniel Webster with the request that the Attorney General present them to the Court for entry on the minutes of their proceedings. This was done the following day and Chief Justice Marshall so ordered, as appeared in the opening pages of Volume VIII of "Peter's Reports." This is the first occasion on which Grandfather's name appears in the United States Supreme Court Reports after his admission to the Bar.

My father, in his "Retrospect of Forty Years," takes William Wirt as an example of how ephemeral the reputation of a lawyer can be. At a reception given at my grandmother's home in New York a few years after Mr. Wirt's death, a young lady picked up a little memento box from the drawing room table. On the box was engraved the inscription:

"A lock of the hair of William Wirt."

She asked father: "Who was William Wirt?"

My father told me long after, that the ignorance of this young woman in regard to the existence of one of the most prominent lawyers of his time taught him a lesson as to the emptiness of professional reputation and even of literary and political fame.

Benjamin F. Butler who became Attorney General in his thirty-seventh year, and was the youngest man ever appointed to that office, had already achieved enviable standing as one of the leading legal and political figures, not only in Albany, his home city, but also in the State of New York. He was born at Kinderhook, Columbia County, New York on December 14th, 1795, of Medad and Hannah Butler. My grandfather had a common school education, studied law in the office of a near neighbor and friend of his family, Martin Van Buren, before that eminent jurist and leading lawyer of Columbia County had entered on his great public career. After my grandfather had been admitted to the Bar Mr. Van Buren took him as his law partner and later they both moved from Kinderhook to Albany where Van Buren & Butler soon became the most prominent firm of lawyers in the Capital of the Empire State. Incidentally Grandfather was District Attorney at Albany from 1821 to 1825.

In 1829 Mr. Van Buren retired from the practice of law to become Secretary of State during President Andrew Jackson's first term. After having served as Vice President Mr. Van Buren himself became President in 1837. Grandfather succeeded to the practice of the law firm of Van Buren & Butler and according to my father's "Retrospect of Forty Years," became "the foremost counsel in the New York Court of Errors and Appeals," having appeared in nine out of the eighteen cases heard during the 1833 term of that court.

In the original edition of the sixth of Peters Reports appears a list of all the gentlemen who were admitted to practice at the Bar of the Supreme Court of the United States at January Term, 1832. On the same page with Grandfather's name is the name of the famous Massachusetts barrister, Rufus Choate. As members of the Supreme Court Bar they were, so to speak, twins. (Later, the custom of listing admissions was discontinued, and reprints of the reports do not include those lists).

There is a story about Rufus Choate, which is here repeated, though the truth of it is not vouched for. However, as Kipling has related, an Indian beggar story-teller, when questioned about the truth of one of his tales, replied: "A good story is always a true story while it is being told."

Rufus Choate, progenitor of the Choate family, so famous in the history of the American Bar, is said to have established as a rule of his office that no legal business should be accepted without a cash retainer fee of at least one hundred dollars. On Mr. Choate's return one day to his office after

BENJAMIN F. BUTLER

MARTIN VAN BUREN

ANDREW JACKSON

appearing in court, his clerk brought him some papers left by a would-be client who desired Mr. Choate to represent him. Having looked over the papers Mr. Choate inquired of the clerk:

"William, did Mr. ——— leave the customary retainer?"

"Well," William replied, "He left only seventy-five dollars."

"That," Mr. Choate declared, "you know is against the rule of the office and very unprofessional."

"But," William explained, "I took all the man had."

"Ah, William," said his employer, "that entirely alters the case—to take all a man has is quite professional."

To paraphrase the statement heard often over the radio, in which the guest speaker's remarks are practically repudiated, in order to protect the broadcasting company or the sponsor:

"The views expressed by Mr. Choate are not necessarily those of the author."

The author, however, qualifies this statement by saying that, never having had the opportunity of taking all a man has, he does not know just what might have happened had such an opportunity come his way.

Nor does this semi-disavowal in any way relate to the historic remark which Mr. Choate made on another occasion and which is quoted by Glenn Brown on the title page of the first and second volume of his History of the United States Capitol: "We have built no temple except the Capitol; we consult no common oracle but the Constitution."

My grandfather, Peter Augustus Jay, and Henry Seymour were appointed commissioners by the Governor of New York in February 1833 to settle the controversy of half a century's duration as to the boundary line between the State of New York and the State of New Jersey. The three other commissioners who were appointed by the Governor of New Jersey were Theodore Frelinghuysen, James Parker and Lucius Q. C. Elmer.

5

In 1824, less than four years after Grandfather had been admitted to the Bar as a full-fledged Counselor at Law,—as distinguished from an Attorney at Law,*—he was appointed one of the commissioners to revise The Statute Laws of the State of New York. The other commissioners were former Chancellor James Kent and the then Lieutenant Governor Erastus Root. It was indeed a compliment to a young man not quite twenty-nine years of age to be named by an Act of the Legislature of his State for such an important task and with such eminent men as his colleagues. The compliment was well deserved, for the words, *"finis opus coronat"* could never be more justly applied than to the work of this commission, in the production of which Grandfather was given the credit of having pulled the laboring oar.

Judge William Kent, son of the great Chancellor, was well aware of the work of the commission and knew how it was allocated among the members. At a memorial meeting of the New York Bar in honor of my grandfather after his death, in 1859, Judge Kent referred to the important part taken by Judge Duer and Mr. Spencer in the operation of the commission. Judge Kent concluded his remarks by saying that "much of the essential excellence of the Revised Statutes, and more of the labor which adapted them to our general system of jurisprudence, the plan and order of the work, the correctness of its style, the learning of the notes, the marginal references, and the admirable index which accompanied it, should be ascribed to the *limae labor*, the patient touches of unwearied art, bestowed by the skill and matchless assiduity of Mr. Butler."

Another speaker described my grandfather's part in drawing up the Revisions as the greatest accomplishment of his life although it was commenced and finished before he was thirty-four years of age. This speaker also told his listeners that prior to his work on the Revision Commission in the first case he argued before the Court of Errors my grandfather

* (*cf.* New York Laws, 1847 ch. 280 §75.)

appearing in court, his clerk brought him some papers left by a would-be client who desired Mr. Choate to represent him. Having looked over the papers Mr. Choate inquired of the clerk:

"William, did Mr. —— leave the customary retainer?"

"Well," William replied, "He left only seventy-five dollars."

"That," Mr. Choate declared, "you know is against the rule of the office and very unprofessional."

"But," William explained, "I took all the man had."

"Ah, William," said his employer, "that entirely alters the case—to take all a man has is quite professional."

To paraphrase the statement heard often over the radio, in which the guest speaker's remarks are practically repudiated, in order to protect the broadcasting company or the sponsor:

"The views expressed by Mr. Choate are not necessarily those of the author."

The author, however, qualifies this statement by saying that, never having had the opportunity of taking all a man has, he does not know just what might have happened had such an opportunity come his way.

Nor does this semi-disavowal in any way relate to the historic remark which Mr. Choate made on another occasion and which is quoted by Glenn Brown on the title page of the first and second volume of his History of the United States Capitol: "We have built no temple except the Capitol; we consult no common oracle but the Constitution."

My grandfather, Peter Augustus Jay, and Henry Seymour were appointed commissioners by the Governor of New York in February 1833 to settle the controversy of half a century's duration as to the boundary line between the State of New York and the State of New Jersey. The three other commissioners who were appointed by the Governor of New Jersey were Theodore Frelinghuysen, James Parker and Lucius Q. C. Elmer.

5

The same subjects referred to this joint commission had already been dealt with by two former commissions without result. This third commission, however, actually accomplished the complete settlement of the controversy over the boundary line between New York and New Jersey, and also other questions affecting the jurisdiction of these States over the Port of New York. As related in the "Retrospect of Forty Years," what was done by this commission "has ever since controlled the jurisdiction and rights of the two States."

The convention adopted bears the date of September 16th, 1833, and was confirmed by Congress June 28, 1834.*

The amending treaty of 1921 † and the legislation of the two States based thereon which established The Port Authority of New York were described, in an address by one of the State officials at the opening of the George Washington Bridge over the Hudson River, as based "on the safe and sound foundations of the Treaty of 1834."

Although assured of election as United States Senator in 1833 my grandfather, highly as he esteemed the office, declined to accept. He thus carried out a resolution, announced at an earlier date, that he would not accept any political office not in line with the profession he had chosen.

True to his native county in 1818 Grandfather had married Harriet Allen of the city of Hudson. She was a sister of that gallant officer of the United States Navy, William Howard Allen, who while in command of the sloop *Alligator*, was killed in an engagement with West Indian pirates. On the monument erected by the city of Hudson in his honor, are graven the words of the last stanza of the poem by Fitz-Greene Halleck commemorating this naval hero:

> "Pride of his country's banded chivalry,
>   His fame their hope, his name their battle cry,
> He lived as mothers wish their sons to live,
> He died as fathers wish their sons to die."

* (1834 Stat. 708.)
† (42 Stat. 174.)

6

Years later a United States naval destroyer was named for William Henry Allen and William Howard Allen, two officers of the United States Navy who were not related, but had at times served together. At the launching in Bath, Maine, the ship was jointly christened by a descendant of William Henry Allen and a great-grand-niece of William Howard Allen—my own niece, Harriet Allen Butler. My share in the ceremony was the recitation of Fitz-Greene Halleck's entire poem.

The *Allen* has been scrapped. The brass plate bearing her name, however, and the reasons for giving it, were saved from the junk pile and presented to our family by a naval officer having authority to do so. The plate, about fifteen inches square, now occupies an honored place on the wall of the library of the Butler family homestead at Yonkers, New York. There also is preserved the original commission of our great-uncle William Howard Allen as an officer of the United States Navy. It is attached to a shield on which hang the sash, sword and epaulets worn by him when he received his fatal wounds.

My great-uncle has been referred to at length because my father was christened after him with the full name of William Howard Allen Butler. This name he used until, at a later period of his professional career, he dropped the "Howard."

Marriage to Harriet Allen, of the city of Hudson, gave my grandfather not only a loving companion until her lamented death in 1853, but the great moral support of a loyal helpmate to assist him in achieving the goals for which he aspired.

Fortunately the same may be said as to the married life not only of Grandfather but also of his son, his grandson and his great-grandson. It cannot be doubted that each of them largely owed or owes whatever success he may have gained to the constancy, faithfulness and loyalty of the helpmate chosen in his youth.

7

In 1824, less than four years after Grandfather had been admitted to the Bar as a full-fledged Counselor at Law,—as distinguished from an Attorney at Law,*—he was appointed one of the commissioners to revise The Statute Laws of the State of New York. The other commissioners were former Chancellor James Kent and the then Lieutenant Governor Erastus Root. It was indeed a compliment to a young man not quite twenty-nine years of age to be named by an Act of the Legislature of his State for such an important task and with such eminent men as his colleagues. The compliment was well deserved, for the words, *"finis opus coronat"* could never be more justly applied than to the work of this commission, in the production of which Grandfather was given the credit of having pulled the laboring oar.

Judge William Kent, son of the great Chancellor, was well aware of the work of the commission and knew how it was allocated among the members. At a memorial meeting of the New York Bar in honor of my grandfather after his death, in 1859, Judge Kent referred to the important part taken by Judge Duer and Mr. Spencer in the operation of the commission. Judge Kent concluded his remarks by saying that "much of the essential excellence of the Revised Statutes, and more of the labor which adapted them to our general system of jurisprudence, the plan and order of the work, the correctness of its style, the learning of the notes, the marginal references, and the admirable index which accompanied it, should be ascribed to the *limae labor,* the patient touches of unwearied art, bestowed by the skill and matchless assiduity of Mr. Butler."

Another speaker described my grandfather's part in drawing up the Revisions as the greatest accomplishment of his life although it was commenced and finished before he was thirty-four years of age. This speaker also told his listeners that prior to his work on the Revision Commission in the first case he argued before the Court of Errors my grandfather

* (*cf.* New York Laws, 1847 ch. 280 §75.)

8

had shown his great ability as a lawyer. It was an important case, involving an abstruse question of law in which he was associated with Aaron Burr and Mr. Van Buren. He was opposed by Mr. Henry, well known as one of the distinguished lawyers of Albany. My grandfather's argument was so complete and thorough that his eminent associates declined to say anything. The case was left on his opening argument and decided in his favor.

The same speaker said further:

"In 1825 the Revisers, who had been appointed by the law of 1824, not having entered on their duties, another law was passed, by which Mr. Butler, Mr. Duer, and Mr. Wheaton (whose place was soon afterwards filled by Mr. Spencer), were appointed commissioners to revise the Statute Laws of the State. The selection of Mr. Butler, then so recently admitted as Counsellor at Law, carried with it evidence of the high estimation in which he was held by the Legislature. His was an undertaking of great hazard to professional reputation, as well as a great labor. It necessarily involved, for a time, the almost entire sacrifice of his business, as he was obliged to devote himself exclusively to that duty. It was a most toilsome and difficult task. But he did not shrink from it. He undertook it; and notwithstanding the prejudices which it at first encountered, it was carried through to a very successful termination."

About sixty years after the Revision had been completed, in January 1889, my father presented to the Bar Association of the City of New York, oil portraits of the three principal Revisers: Judge John Duer, Judge John C. Spencer and my grandfather. Chancellor Kent, Mr. Wheaton and Lieutenant Governor Root as co-commissioners served only for brief periods.

My father's presentation address on "The Revision and the Revisers" was published as a separate volume by the Bar Association and distributed to the members as an expression of thanks and appreciation.

In his "Retrospect of Forty Years" my father refers to the "Revision" as "one of the most important legal works in the nineteenth century—a novel, bold and successful attempt to bring the whole common law of England and all existing Colonial and State Statutes affecting our Commonwealth [New York] into a complete and systematic code based upon scientific principles and sufficient for all the needs of the Government."

The many tributes received after my father's address before the Bar Association of the City of New York, from eminent judges and jurists, bore out to the fullest extent his estimate of the value of the Revised Statutes which, as he expressed it, "became the models of the Statute Law of the States of the Union and remain today [1889] the groundwork of our existing system of Statutory Law." After my grandfather's return to practice from the Attorney-Generalship, Governor Hamilton Fish of New York asked him to serve on a commission to codify the general law of the State. My grandfather declined this honor, yet it is not known whether his declination was due to inability to devote his time to the task, or because, agreeing with many of the legal profession, including the author, he did not believe in the codification of the Common Law.

It is impossible in a sketch of this nature completely to recount all the incidents of the work of my grandfather in connection with the revision of the Statute Law of New York in which he took such an active part. His "Notes of the Reporter," consisting of a number of pamphlets relating to the various subjects of the revision, were bound in six volumes and came into my possession after my father's death in 1902. In 1911 a destructive fire in the State Capitol at Albany damaged beyond repair many volumes of the State Law Library including its only set of these notes. The State Librarian wrote to all the descendants of the revisers whom he could locate, asking for a set of the notes to replace the one destroyed in the fire. He obtained my set as a gift to the State and told me that it was much more complete than the one lost in the fire.

Quoting the "Revision and the Revisers" we learn:

The original text of the entire Revised Statutes supplemented by the Act of Legislature of the State of New York December 10, 1828—by which they were enacted as the Statutory Law of the State—is contained in one folio volume printed for the Legislature of 1828 by Packard and Van Benthuysen of Albany. It is a noble specimen of the typographical art almost rivaling the famous classics of Baskerville. A few copies are extant.

The copy of this "noble specimen" of the art of printing originally belonged to my grandfather and later came into my possession. Considering however that it was really a family heirloom, it was presented by me to the Library of Congress in Washington in 1931. It remains there with an appropriate inscription placed upon it by the Librarian.

President Andrew Jackson's invitation to Grandfather to become his Attorney General was conveyed in a letter written by Vice President Martin Van Buren. In the letter Mr. Van Buren explained that while the emoluments of the office were not great, there would be opportunities to add to his income by continuing to engage in private practice. Evidently there were some such opportunities although they probably did not produce the financial results attributed to Daniel Webster's frequent appearances in the Supreme Court of the United States. The pertinent part of Mr. Van Buren's letter to my grandfather reads as follows:

Although you are not the slave of mad ambition, you are as you ought to be, tenacious of your professional standing. That cannot be *increased* at home, and can only be made *national* by becoming identified with national concerns. Depend upon it, my dear sir, that this is so.

The fact presses itself upon my observation almost daily, when I find how little is known, or cared, abroad, about you who are at the very top of the ladder at home. Mr. Wirt, Mr. Webster, Mr. Pinckney, and Mr. Taney, although possessing the same talents, would not have gone beyond a passing observation, out

11

of their own States if they had not entered upon the national theatre. . . . The reason why this is so, it is unnecessary to go into; the fact is sufficient, and undeniable, that the great body of the people will only look for the great men of the *Nation* amongst those who are actually engaged in its service. Although you are too wise to be craving for a distinction of this sort, you are at the same time too wise to be indifferent to it. Providence has cut you out for its acquisition in this very place, and you have no right to turn back upon the occasion, which presents it to you, in so honorable and entirely unexceptionable a manner.

In a pecuniary point of view, it cannot, I deliberately think be otherwise than beneficial. The salary is $4,500, besides office, messenger, clerks, etc., and occasional compensation from the Government for services which do not necessarily appertain to the office. You can enter upon the business of the Supreme Court of U. S. with advantages, which if not immediately equal to those of Webster, (who makes his thousands not to say tens of thousands by it), they very soon would be; and the President says it will be competent for you, without prejudice to the public interest, to attend the higher courts at N. York and Albany. All previous Atty. Genls. who desired it have done so in respect to their own States.

To the former place you will next season be able to go in 15 hours, and to the latter in a day and a night. What then is there to prevent you from increasing your provision for your children which I admit to be obligatory on you? Nothing, that I can see. You can live as cheap here as in N. York. Your manner of living can be regulated by your own taste, and as everybody knows that you are not a man of pleasure and parade, nobody will gossip about you. By taking this course, you will accomplish what you are also anxious about, viz., that you can be more with your family than heretofore. The only exception need be, your visits to N. York during the sittings of the Court, when you can take your family with you, without stopping between this and N. Y.—especially when the railroad, the making of which is now under full operation, is completed.

Referring to Mr. Van Buren's allusion to the expected improvement in transportation, Father used to tell us that, as a small boy while he was playing one day in his father's office in their Albany home, a visitor entered and excitedly exclaimed to his father:

12

Smith Thompson

John Marshall

FELIX GRUNDY

JOSEPH STORY

"Butler, they have just put on another coach to New York and they may put another on for Buffalo. You and I will not live to see it, but this boy (pointing to Father) will live to see the day when we shall have a daily coach between Albany and Rochester."

That small boy probably did not remember whether or not there ever was a daily coach between Albany and Rochester, but he did live to see the day when, while living in Yonkers on the Hudson, he argued one case before the Court of Appeals in Albany, and another before the Supreme Court of the United States in Washington, and all within three days. Had he made such a prediction to his father's visitor, the excited Albanian would have expressed his fear that friend Butler's son was a simpleton.

Present day facilities for transportation of body and transportation of sight and of sound have so far progressed, and they surely will continue to do so, that it is impossible to predict how soon any one point on the globe may be reached from any other point. With the rapid development of the telephone, radio, and television, the time may not be far off when we shall not be obliged as now to present our cases to the courts personally, but may do so without leaving our offices or even our homes. In fact even the judges may not have to leave their homes to listen to our arguments or actually to attend conferences with one another to decide which one of us has failed to convince them of the justice of our client's cause.

At frequent intervals in volumes eighth to twelfth inclusive of Peters Reports the name of Benjamin F. Butler appears as representing the Government in a number of cases. In many of these he was successful. In not a few however the Court does not seem to have adopted the views of the Attorney General.

In running through Peters Reports it was rather strange to a New Yorker to find cases in which occur such now

13

familiar names as Phelps, Dodge and Company.* That well known firm was party to a tariff case one hundred years ago, the merits of which were not involved in the Supreme Court proceeding, but only a continuance of the trial of the tariff case. Evidently at the instance of the New York District Attorney, the Attorney General of the United States vainly sought to have the Supreme Court set aside postponement granted by the court below.

My grandfather was unsuccessful in his first recorded case.† This was against Tench Ringgold, a famous, some say notorious, character in the District of Columbia, who built the house at Nineteenth and F Street which in later years was occupied by Chief Justice Melville Weston Fuller.

Speaking of "notorious" reminds me of an incident that happened at Saratoga in 1886. While standing with my father, who was then President of the American Bar Association, on the front porch of the Grand Union Hotel, two men accosted us. One of them asked Father if he would kindly tell him his name and who he was. On Father's replying that he was William Allen Butler of the New York Bar and President of the American Bar Association, the inquirer turned to his companion, and in a voice of triumph exclaimed:

"There, I told you he was somebody notorious."

Father always enjoyed the joke, maintaining that at last someone had accurately described him right to his face.

Another early case of my grandfather's involved the determination of the nature of the contents of 112 casks which the Government insisted fell within the technical tariff definition of "sugar." ‡ As the result however of its dilution with something else, the Court refused to include the contents of the casks within the tariff definition. Evidently the method of escaping payment of duties and taxes not by illegally evading, but by legally avoiding, being within the legal definition of the article taxed, is not a new feature

* (8 Peters 700.)   † (8 Peters 150.)   ‡ (8 Peters 277.)

14

with which Congress has to grapple in establishing subjects and rates for taxation.

The tenth of Peters Reports begins with an account of the death of Chief Justice John Marshall, which occurred in Philadelphia on July 6, 1835. It was followed by a motion made by Henry Clay which was granted by the Court on January 12, 1836, to have the proceedings of the meeting of the Bar of the Supreme Court entered on the records of the Court. Also recorded were the remarks of Mr. Justice Story who, presiding as the senior justice, accepted the motion.

In a contest of legal strategy my grandfather seems to have bested Daniel Webster by sustaining the discontinuance of a non-Governmental case from the State of Maine in the Supreme Court, thus avoiding a decision against his client, which would probably have been embarrassing in other pending litigation.* In the same volume of Peters Reports however, there is record of a case in which Mr. Webster got the best of Mr. Butler in a question involving admissibility of evidence.†

Nor was my grandfather successful in the Skiddy Case. As Attorney General he endeavored—under the non-importation Slave Act of 1818—to send back on their return to this country persons of color who had left the State of the Union in which they and their masters resided. The Court, by Chief Justice Taney, held that the act did not apply to persons of color brought back by their masters from a temporary sojourn abroad.‡

Probably my grandfather was not greatly disappointed when the Court did not reverse a judgment of a lower court which was adverse to the United States by relieving a government official who had a clean record, from liability on an account with the Treasurer of the United States which he

* (Veazie v. Wadleigh. 11 Peters 55.)
† (U.S. v. Leffler. 11 Peters 86.)
‡ (U.S. v. Skiddy. 11 Peters 73.)

claimed to have paid, but which could not be proved because all the records in the Treasury showing such payment had been destroyed by fire.

In another case my grandfather obtained a decision to the effect that a corporation was to be regarded as a *person* within the meaning of the statute involved.[*] This is only referred to here as a question which was then a novel one, but which has long since been settled. He also succeeded in having the jurisdiction of the Federal Court sustained in a criminal prosecution for theft on the high seas.[†] This question the lower court had failed to agree upon.

As Attorney General my grandfather argued many appeals in cases involving tracts of land within territories ceded by foreign countries to the United States. Such land was claimed to have become the private property of individuals before the cession, and their rights were protected by the treaty under which the United States had acquired the territory containing the lands claimed. In some of these cases the titles of the claimants were sustained, but in others the claims were shown not to be well-founded and thus large areas were declared to be public lands of the United States.[‡]

In a case in which he appeared not as Attorney General, but as personal counsel, my grandfather represented Marguerite, "a woman of color of Missouri." [§] After several trials and mistrials in the State Courts, she had obtained a verdict against a man for ill-treating her and holding her in prison. Having been defeated in the State Court on his contention that the woman was a slave in his lawful possession and so could be detained by him, this man made an effort to have the Supreme Court review the decision. The contention on behalf of the woman that the judgment

[*] (Beaston v. Farmers Bank of Delaware. 12 Peters 102.)
[†] (U.S. v. Coombs. 12 Peters 72.)
[‡] (U.S. v. Mills Heirs. 12 Peters 215; U.S. v. Kingsley. 12 Peters 476; Delassus v. U.S. 9 Peters 117; Chouteau's Heirs v. U.S. 9 Peters 137.)
[§] (Choteau v. Marguerite. 12 Peters 507.)

WILLIAM ALLEN BUTLER

MORRISON R. WAITE

ROGER B. TANEY

of the State Court holding her to be a free woman and not a slave, because based on State Law, was held not to be reviewable by the Supreme Court of the United States. This contention was sustained in an opinion by Mr. Justice Story who dismissed the case. This dismissal amounted to an affirmation of the judgment of the State Court in favor of my grandfather's client.

This case involved the construction of the clauses in the Louisiana Purchase Treaty protecting the inhabitants of the ceded territory in their property rights. The opposing counsel Francis Scott Key and Senator Benton contended that these clauses included slaves. My grandfather's contention however was that the State Court by its verdict had held that, although Marguerite's mother was an Indian captured by the French prior to the cession and held as a slave, the daughter was not a slave, and the decision of the State Court was beyond the jurisdiction of the Supreme Court to review.

A few pages later in the same volume we find my grandfather as Attorney General and Mr. Key on the same side opposing Mr. Cox and Mr. Johnson in a very important case.* It involved the power of the lower court to issue, as it had done, a writ of mandamus to compel a Postmaster General to carry out the provisions of an Act of Congress and to pay the parties in whose favor the writ had been issued, the amount found in a proceeding to be due them by the Solicitor of the Treasury. The Government fought against the issuance of the mandamus and took the case to the Supreme Court where it was elaborately argued. The abstracts of the argument and the opinions fill 130 pages of the twelfth of Peters Reports.

The Supreme Court held against the Government and sustained the power of the lower court to issue the mandamus. Mr. Justice Smith Thompson delivered the opinion. Chief

* (Kendall v. U.S. 12 Peters 524.)

Justice Taney, however, dissented in a long opinion in which Justices Catron and Barbour concurred.

In his opinion Mr. Justice Thompson said:

"It was urged at the Bar that the Postmaster General was alone subject to the direction and control of the President, with respect to the execution of the duty imposed upon him by this law; and this right of the President is claimed, as growing out of the obligation imposed upon him by the Constitution to take care that the laws be faithfully executed. This is a doctrine that cannot receive the sanction of this court. It would be vesting in the President a dispensing power, which has no countenance for its support in any part of the Constitution: and is asserting a principle, which, if carried out in its results, to all cases falling within it, would be clothing the President with a power entirely to control the legislation of Congress, and paralyze the administration of justice."

The above is quoted at length as being an interesting item in view of what is occurring at the present time.

Three or four years after the delivery of this opinion, my grandfather evidently asked Mr. Justice Thompson something about the foregoing paragraph. They had been friends since before the Justice was appointed to the bench. The Justice replied in a letter which is interesting because of a statement made in it that after Justice Thompson "had read the opinion of the Court you [B. F. B.] disclaimed what I had imputed to the counsel on the argument relative to the power of the President under that provision of the Constitution."

The letter, which was inserted by my father in the volume containing the record of the case, was as follows:

New York, January 4th, 1841

Dear Sir:

In answer to your letter of the 24th ult. in relation to what occurred in the Supreme Court in the case of Kendall vs. the United States I have to state, that after I had read the opinion of the Court, as prepared by me you disclaimed, what I had imputed to the Counsel on the argument, relative to the power of the President under that provision in the constitution, which imposes upon him the duty of taking care that the laws be faithfully executed. At this distance of time, I do not recollect distinctly what fell from other members of the Court. All, however, concurred in opinion, that the argument had been urged at the bar, upon that question, as stated in the opinion. It is not usual in preparing an opinion, when reference is made to the argument of Counsel, to designate by name, by whom it was used. In preparing the opinion however, I alluded to the argument of your associate Counsel. I had therefore no hesitation in stating from the Bench, that I did not mean to refer to you, but to your associate, by whom the argument had been pressed with considerable earnestness in the manner represented in the opinion. How this was understood by the other Judges I know not.

I am, very respectfully,
Your Obedient Servant,
Smith Thompson.

B. F. Butler, Esq.

Chapter II

LATER CAREER OF MY GRANDFATHER

THE FOREGOING is interesting as throwing a sidelight on the proceedings of the Court a century ago. It seems evident that my grandfather's disclaimer must have been made in the courtroom after Justice Thompson had read his opinion.

How much more interesting would it not be to those who assemble in the courtroom on Monday mornings to hear the Court announce its opinions if counsel, especially those who have been listening to adverse opinions, could rise and comment on the views of the Court as expressed by the justices delivering the opinions.

This reminds me of a personal experience in which a commission—a quasi-judicial tribunal—declined to take jurisdiction of claims for a large amount presented by my law firm. One of the five commissioners with whom three others united delivered the opinion. The remaining commissioner wrote a dissenting opinion in which he stated that "it was as clear as the noonday sun that jurisdiction existed and should be exercised."

The statute establishing the commission provided that, in cases of doubt the commission could certify the questions involved to the Supreme Court of the United States. A motion was made for such certification. After hearing my argument in favor of granting the certificate and the argument of the Assistant Attorney General against granting the certificate, the presiding Commissioner expressed the view that the motion should be denied. Addressing me he said:

20

"Mr. Butler, is there any doubt expressed in the majority opinion as to our lack of jurisdiction?"

My answer was of course: "No, your Honor."

"Well, Mr. Butler, the minority opinion says that 'our jurisdiction is clear as the noonday sun.' There is no doubt in that, is there?"

Of course there was not.

"Very well then," he said, "we cannot certify there is a question of doubt and must deny your motion."

Just what may have been my remarks induced by this remarkable decision has passed from my memory. But the observation of the presiding commissioner has remained. We had known each other many years.

"My dear Butler," he said, "we are all very fond of you and we know that you must be greatly disappointed by this decision. Far be it from me to question the constitutional privilege of every defeated lawyer to swear at the Court, but really don't you yourself think that the swearing ought to be done at the corner grocery and not in the courtroom?"

This very kindly reproach resulted in my disclaiming any intention of swearing at, or even criticizing the Court. Perhaps however something that I said may have let the commissioners know my judgment of one of the most ridiculous decisions ever pronounced.

Reading the quoted paragraphs in the opinion of Justice Thompson together with those in my grandfather's letter does make one wonder just how forcefully my grandfather expressed his disclaimer to the Court. It may be that he meant more than his words indicated.

Father used to tell of a client who called on him about a case in which he had been served with a bill of complaint. He said that the document had been shown to my grandfather, who told him to bring it to the office for further attention. In answer to my father's inquiry as to what his father had thought of the bill of complaint, the client replied, much to father's surprise, who knew that such language could not have been used—

"Why, he said it was the G-d d---dest bill he had ever seen in his whole life."

"Oh no," said Father, "he could not have said that."

"Well," said the client, "I can't just remember exactly what he did say, but that was exactly what he meant."

Perhaps neither my grandfather nor myself knew just how far we went in our "disclaimers." The Court however evidently did know what we meant. Whether he ever exercised his constitutional right to swear at the Court—as dissenting opinions would have justified him in doing—is unknown; but my right to do so was exercised to the fullest extent, not necessarily in any corner grocery, but wherever an audience, outside the courtroom and sufficiently interested, could be found.

In October 1836 my grandfather received an urgent request from President Jackson to fill the office of Secretary of War. It had been vacated because its incumbent, General Lewis Cass, was sent as our Minister to France. In a personal letter the President said:

"I rely upon your taking charge of that department until the 4th of March next. This combined with your duty as Attorney General will be onerous, still I know your capacity and indefatigable industry, competent to both, and as far as my abilities and health will permit, the burden shall be lightened. Please present me kindly to your amiable lady and family, and accept the assurance of my continued respect, confidence and esteem."

According to our family tradition, the portfolio of the Secretary of War was not forthwith accepted because of Grandmother's opposition. She was, as were also my maternal grandparents, of good old Nantucket Quaker stock with an ingrained aversion to war. As the story goes, when urged not to object to Grandfather's acceptance of the offer, she said:

"Frank,"—so he was called by members of his family, using his middle name—"may not have to go to war himself and kill anybody, but he may have to give orders that will make somebody else kill someone, and that is just as bad as though he did it himself."

How her objections were overcome does not appear, but eventually her husband was confirmed as Secretary of War. As there is no record either of his killing anybody himself, or of his ordering anyone to kill anybody else, Grandmother's fears do not seem to have been realized.

He was confirmed by the Senate on March 3, 1837 just before President Jackson's term expired, and he occupied the post for several months on the President's Commission. His confirmation was the result of a special message sent to the Senate. Otherwise as a Presidential appointee his commission would have expired with the end of the President's term of office.

In "History of the Cabinet of the United States" by William Henry Smith it is stated that "Benjamin F. Butler has the unique distinction of holding at the same time two Cabinet positions under appointment by the President and confirmation by the Senate."

One of his portraits hangs in the Department of Justice and another in the Department of War.

My grandfather continued as Attorney General and as Secretary of War only until Mr. Van Buren's candidate for Secretary of War, Joel R. Poinsett, returned from Mexico where he had been the United States Minister. Incidentally, the flower which so profusely and beautifully adorns our homes during Christmas week, originated in Mexico and is said to have been named "poinsettia" as a Mexican national compliment to the popular wife of the American Minister.

Attorney General Butler not only wrote many opinions, but wrote them himself. In those days Assistant Attorney Generals, so numerous now, were wholly unknown. His opinions fill 145 pages of the second volume of the published opinions of the Attorney General, and 371 of the third volume. During the five years that he occupied the office, numerous questions were referred to him by the President and by his fellow members of the Cabinet. Some of them involved questions of constitutional law which had not hitherto arisen.

One of his opinions, dated February 3, 1838, relates to the establishment of the $5,000,000 removal fund for the benefit of the Cherokee Indians.*

The proper application of this fund is still the subject of litigation in the Court of Claims. Recently there was occasion to investigate it by my law firm of Butler & Butler, composed of a grandson and a great-grandson of the Attorney General who wrote that opinion more than a century ago.

Regarding the relative powers and functions of the President in making appointments to office and the Senate's power in confirming them, Arthur Krock, head of the Washington Bureau of the New York *Times,* wrote in one of his dispatches:

"The Senate's powers as thus set down have not been questioned for many years. In 1837 the Attorney General [Benjamin F. Butler] interpreted the appointive power as follows. 'The Senate cannot originate an appointment. Its constitutional action is confined to the simple affirmation or rejection of the President's nominations, and such nominations fail whenever it rejects them. The Senate may suggest conditions and limitations to the President, but it cannot vary those submitted by him, for no appointment can be made except on his nomination, agreed to without qualification or alteration.'" †

The opinion related to the appointment of a naval officer which the Senate had confirmed with a qualification as to how he should rank. The Attorney General advised the

* (3 Op. Attorney General 304.)
† (3 Op. Attorney General 188, 189.)

Secretary of the Navy, who had propounded the question, that no commission could be issued thereunder. This opinion, after citing several precedents concludes as follows:

"The last one [precedent] illustrates the propriety and advantage of a strict adherence to the provisions of the Constitution in the exercise of the appointing power. The harmony of the two co-ordinate branches, the independence of the President, the just weight of the Senate, and the useful operation of the power itself, will no doubt, be best secured by confining each branch to its peculiar functions and not allowing either to deviate from the order of procedure prescribed by the Constitution."

This concise statement of the relations of the co-ordinate branches of the Federal Government under the Constitution is as appropriate today in regard to existing events as it was when this opinion was delivered over a century ago by Attorney General Butler. His son, grandson and great-grandson have all spoken, written and argued in support of principles enunciated in the document described by Gladstone as "the most wonderful work ever struck off at a given time by the brain and purpose of man." It is not only the cornerstone, but the bulwark of our national government.

Whether or not his descendants have inherited my grandfather's legal ability, the same newspaper that cited his opinion of 1838 bears witness to the fact that his direct successors at the Bar of the Supreme Court have not only inherited but have expressed views similar to those of their ancestor in regard to the Constitution of the United States. The New York *Times* of February 5, 1890 published an editorial on my father's address at the morning exercises of the Supreme Court Centennial Celebration. It commended his able exposition of the judiciary provisions of the Constitution, and his tribute to the Supreme Court. In 1902 the same newspaper complimented me by a review written by John Bassett Moore of my book on the "Treaty-Making Power of the United States." In that work Mr. Gladstone's above quoted statement is referred to as reflecting my own views in regard to the Constitution. In May 1939 the New York *Times* published a column account of a unanimous decision of the Supreme Court of the United States which, as set forth in an opinion by Chief Justice Hughes, sustained the contention urged by my son, Henry F. Butler, in support of the sacredness of the birthright of American citizenship given by the Constitution to those born within the United States or under its jurisdiction.*

After resigning as Attorney General, my grandfather did not return to Albany, but established himself in New York where he soon became one of the leaders of the Bar of that city and so continued until his death in 1858.

At the request of President Van Buren he served as District Attorney for the Southern District of New York from December 1838 until March 1841 when his successor, Ogden Hoffman, qualified. At the request of President Polk he served a second time from March 1845 until September 1848. In neither case was his acceptance the result of a desire to hold office but to comply with the wishes of the Chief Executives who appointed him, and who wished to have a man directing the legal affairs of the nation in the greatest commercial center of the country in whom perfect confidence could be placed.

As a delegate to the Democratic Convention at Baltimore in 1844, my grandfather led Mr. Van Buren's adherents for the Presidential nomination. When it became evident, however, that with the help of the two-thirds rule and what my father's "Retrospect" describes as "the conspiracy of the Southern leaders" of the convention, his adversaries could and would defeat him, my grandfather withdrew Mr. Van Buren's name in accordance with preconvention arrangements between his leader and himself. This resulted in the nomination of James K. Polk who was subsequently elected, defeating Henry Clay of Kentucky.

* (Perkins v. Elg, 325 U.S. 307.)

26

While the Convention was in session Samuel F. B. Morse sent the first telegraphic message "What hath God wrought." This was immediately followed by the first telegraphic news

---

These volumes are dedicated
with affection and respect
to the memory of my grandfather
BENJAMIN FRANKLIN BUTLER
whom the Historian Bancroft described
as "ever the upright statesman."
He was born at Kinderhook Landing (Stuyvesant)
New York, December 14, 1795, and
died at Paris, France, November 8, 1858.
He was appointed in 1824 a Commissioner to Revise the
Statute Laws of the State of New York.
He was Attorney-General of the United States from 1833
to 1838 during the administrations of ANDREW
JACKSON and MARTIN VAN BUREN, and for a part of
that period he was also Secretary of War.
On more than one occasion, while he was Attorney-
General, he sustained
THE TREATY-MAKING POWER OF THE UNITED STATES
before the
SUPREME COURT
while JOHN MARSHALL was the CHIEF JUSTICE
and JOSEPH STORY an ASSOCIATE JUSTICE
of that august tribunal.
"There were giants in the earth in those days."

DEDICATION OF AUTHOR'S BOOK ON TREATY MAKING POWER
OF THE UNITED STATES

message, which announced Mr. Polk's nomination and was sent from Baltimore to Washington. This was the beginning of the wonderful systems of transmission of news not only throughout this country, but all over the world. Not long afterward, to local telegraph systems were added the great chains of ocean cables, brought into being by the tireless work of Cyrus W. Field. His brother Stephen J. Field sat on the Bench of the Supreme Court of the United States for a longer period than any other Justice. He exceeded the term of Chief Justice Marshall and also that of Justice Harlan.*

My father often told us about his father's efforts while Attorney General to obtain sufficient office and clerical help to carry on the duties of his post. In the address of Attorney General Cummings delivered at the dedication ceremony in 1934 of the new Department of Justice Building in Washington, there was confirmation of all that we had heard on that point. Congratulating him on his very interesting history of the organization of the Department of Justice and its housing, I told him how just a century before the Department moved into this new building with more than a thousand rooms to accommodate several thousand officers and employees on his staff, my grandfather had to fight to have an additional one-half room added to the single one allotted to him in the War Department Building, and also to have two clerical assistants instead of one.

Attorney General Cummings said in his address: "It is not therefore surprising that the first Attorney General, Edmund Randolph, described himself as 'a sort of mongrel between the State and the United States; called an officer of some rank under the latter and yet thrust out to get a livelihood in the former.'

"On the removal of the seat of government to Washington, while the various departments were housed in nondescript buildings grouped about the President's house, no accommodations were provided for the Attorney General. He was expected to furnish his own quarters, fuel, stationery, and clerk. He was the 'forgotten man' of his day."

* (Field, March 10, 1863-December 1, 1897; Marshall, January 31, 1801-July 6, 1835; Harlan, November 29, 1877-October 14, 1911.)

Nor was the Supreme Court of the United States any better housed in those days than was the Attorney General. This is apparent from my father's account of his first visit to the Court:

"He [Grandfather] led me into the Supreme Courtroom which was then in the basement of the North Wing of the Capitol, the space now [1902] occupied by the Law Library. In the vestibule of this basement are certain marble pillars of grace and beauty, not now often noticed by visitors to the Capitol, who seldom enter at this point. Each column consists of two rows of cornstalks, one surmounting the other, the full grown ears in the open corn-leaves forming the capitals. This is an adaptation of the classical Corinthian order which from an artistic point of view may seem barbaric, but the effect of which to my eye has always been most pleasing, and to my mind most appropriate in associating the highest form of ancient art with a common product of our western continent.

"These columns flank the platform from which rises the marble circular staircase which in 1833, and until wings were added to the Capitol, led to the Senate Chamber. This room is now [1902] occupied by the Supreme Court, which until 1860 was most inadequately housed in the basement, underneath the Senate—an arrangement wholly unjustifiable unless perhaps by the idea that Justice should underlie legislation."

Mr. Justice Harlan had frequently talked to me about those columns designed by Thomas Jefferson which in his opinion were the most beautiful things in the Capitol. When he and Mrs. Harlan celebrated their golden wedding anniversary Mrs. Butler and I were lucky enough to find a set of four Jefferson Column candlesticks, which we had gilded and presented to them in honor of the occasion.

In continuing his account of his first visit to the Supreme Court, my father writes:

"My boyish attention was fastened upon the seven judges as they entered the room—seven being the number then

29

composing the Court. It was a procession of old men—for so they seemed to me—who halted on their way to the bench, each of them taking from a peg hanging on the side of the wall near the entrance a black robe and donning it in full view of the assembled lawyers and other spectators. This somewhat extra-judicial act impressed me more than any subsequent proceeding of the Court, and left a vivid picture in my memory.

"Long afterward when I went to Washington to argue cases before the highest tribunal, contrasting the dignified formalities which attended the opening of the Court at every session with the robing method which I have described, I began to think I must have been mistaken and that I could not have seen Chief Justice Marshall, Judge Story and their associates doing so informal a thing as putting on their robes after entering the courtroom.

"One day after the adjournment of the Court, Chief Justice Taney stopped, as was oftentimes the habit, to exchange a word with me. I seized the opportunity to ask him whether my recollection in this matter of the robing of the Justices was correct or at fault. He said that I was quite right in my remembrance and that until the Court was moved upstairs, 'the Judges always put on their robes in the courtroom.'"

In my father's "Retrospect," already so often alluded to, there is a reference to the 'Albany Regency' of which Martin Van Buren was the head as he was of the political party of which my grandfather was also a member. Mr. Van Buren with Governor Marcy, Edwin Crosswell, Azariah C. Flagg, Silas Wright, John A. Dix, my grandfather and other leading men of Albany, because of their constant union, acquired the sobriquet of the 'Albany Regency' and according to the "Retrospect" they were "maligned as a prototype of 'machine' politicians, but there never was a more groundless charge. They were associated not only for the promotion of party interest, but mainly for the sake of the principles which their party represented. They reaped no pecuniary advantages for themselves from their combination touching public affairs.

"No one of them grew rich or advanced his personal fortune by his connection with the affairs of state. I believe that the unifying force which held them together and made them a power in the State, was the identity of their views as to the true principles of government and the duties imposed upon citizens. Their unselfish and undeviating personal regard for Mr. Van Buren was something remarkable and rare in political friendships. This high gift and faculty of attracting to himself, by strong ties of friendship, able and upright men has been well cited by one of his biographers as a proof of the intrinsic worth of Mr. Van Buren's character."

This opinion of my father in regard to the character of the members of the "Albany Regency" is confirmed by DeAlva S. Alexander who says in his "Political History of the State of New York," published in 1906:

"The appointment of Talcott, Marcy & Butler changed the existing political system . . . and the Regency was destined to continue many years, and to number among its members men of character and great influence. But the men who organized the Regency, giving it power and the respect of the people, by refusing to do what their fine sense of honor did not approve were Talcott, Marcy & Butler. It was as remarkable a trio as ever sat about a table.

"In the passing of these three great intellects there is something peculiarly touching. Talcott died suddenly at the early age of 45, leaving the members of the New York Bar as sincere mourners. Butler, after highest and purest living, died at 59 just as he landed in France to visit the scene of which he had read and dreamed.* Marcy, at 62 having recently retired as President Pierce's Secretary of State, was found lifeless, lying upon his bed, book in hand.

* This is an error. Benjamin F. Butler died at 63. C.H.B.

31

He had been reading, as he had read since childhood, whenever there came a lull in the demand for his wisdom, his counsel, and his friendship."

The "Dictionary of American Biography" says in regard to my grandfather's withdrawal from public official life:

"He might have had his pick of Cabinet posts under Van Buren, but the practice of the law appealed more strongly to him than political office. Nor could President Polk persuade him seven years later to re-enter the Cabinet as Secretary of War. . . . The last ten years of his life he devoted entirely to the law. . . . His rank among the leaders of the Bar was firmly established. Chancellor Kent spoke of him as 'this remarkable lawyer whose memoranda the student finds in all his books.'

"Butler's interest in the law as a science led him to organize a Department of Law in the University of the City of New York in 1838 and to serve for several years as its leading professor. In politics he was a staunch Jacksonian Democrat. He headed the Electoral College of New York which cast its vote for Polk in 1845. As the contest over slavery grew more heated, however, he began to waver. He supported his old chief Van Buren when he ran on the Free Soil Ticket in 1848, but returned to the Democratic fold in 1852 to vote for Pierce and the finality of the Compromise Act in 1852.

"The Kansas-Nebraska Act of 1854 drove him out of the Democratic ranks. With thousands of other anti-Nebraska Democrats, he joined the new Republican Party and cast his presidential ballot for Fremont in 1856. He appeared at a mass meeting in City Hall Park, New York City on May 13, 1854 to denounce the repeal of the Missouri Compromise."

The New York University Law School was very dear to my grandfather's heart as was everything connected with that institution to our family. His younger brother, Charles, was on the council for more than fifty years and was its president for more than twenty-five years. My father also was on

THE SUPREME COURT OF THE UNITED STATES

(from Harper's Weekly, January 28, 1888)

SALMON P. CHASE

SCOTLAND LIGHTSHIP

Reproduced from photographic print of Lightship Number 20 which occupied the Scotland Lightship station but which was, at the time the photograph was taken, stationed at Cross Rip. Reproduced by courtesy of Lieutenant Commander G. B. Gelly, U.S.C.G.

its council and for many years was its president. The warmest expression of commendation with regard to the Law School came from Mr. Justice Story, in his reply to the copy of the opening address sent to him by my grandfather.

There can be no more fitting conclusion to this sketch of my grandfather's life than by quoting in condensed form, the last few pages of the address delivered by my father on the presentation of the portraits of the Revisers of the Statute Laws of the State of New York to the Bar Association of the City of New York. On that occasion he said that his father to the end of his life had hoped for a peaceful solution by constitutional methods.

"His words—'never despair of the right. Tyrants, and apostates may attempt what they please. They may endeavor to bear down the rights of the people, but all their assaults will be in vain in the presence of a free, intelligent people like those of the Free States,' were prophetic of results reached in a way that he did not foresee. Like the Scriptural portion accorded to the good man, he was 'taken away from the evil to come.'"

Quoting further from the same address:

"The later years of his professional life were largely given as counsel in litigations of great importance in one of which some English capitalists were represented by him in association with Charles O'Connor, William Kent, and William Curtis Noyes and opposed by Greene C. Bronson, Samuel Beardsley, and Nicholas Hill. So important was this case that the Court of Appeals as shown in the fifteenth volume of its Reports, gave an entire term to its hearing, and probably no such forensic contest ever occurred in or is likely to occur in New York Courts.

"In spite of his exhausted strength and failing health, he was induced to enter upon another case, which proved to be his final professional contest, in which his personal sympathies and sense of justice were enlisted in behalf of a client whose cause he espoused as if it were his own.

"Uriah P. Levy, a captain of the United States Navy, who had risen in the service by his gallantry and efficiency, had been a comrade in the War of 1812 of Father's brother-in-law, Lieut. William Howard Allen, of whom mention has already been made. They were fellow prisoners in England at one time and the story is told that in order to extend the privilege of walking from their place of confinement to a certain mile-stone they took advantage of the darkness in one of their walks to dig it up and remove it for a considerable distance, thus securing a substantial enlargement of the jail liberties.

"The personality of Levy, who was an Israelite, was not agreeable to his fellow-officers and occasions of complaint and provocation arose wherever he was placed on duty. After a series of court-martials, he was dismissed from the service of the United States, but the sentence was disapproved by President Tyler. The Navy Department failed to assign him to any post of duty and finally his name was stricken from the roll without notice or opportunity to be heard.

"After long and patient effort Congress was induced to institute a Court of Inquiry to investigate the case. After a long and arduous trial with the aid of his counsel, [B.F.B.] Levy made good his claim and was restored to rank with a vindication of character, as complete as it was unique, in the history of the Naval Service.

"This was the last important work done by my father, and is a signal illustration of what may be accomplished, by patience and skill, in reversing wrong judgments and vindicating right principles.

"In 1858, accompanied by his two youngest daughters, my father sailed for Europe and on reaching Paris, was taken ill almost immediately. He died at the Hotel du Louvre, November 8, 1858, aged sixty-two years, ten months and twenty-five days.

"At the meeting of American citizens in Paris on the

occasion of his death, John Y. Mason of Virginia, then United States Minister to France, afterwards conspicuous in the memorable Mason and Slidell incident of the Rebellion, presided, and Hamilton Fish, already eminent in public life, and later a wise and efficient Secretary of State, presented the resolutions. On the eve of their bitter struggle, the North and South united by leading representatives of each section in a tribute of respect to a man justly eulogized by both for his services to his native State and to the whole country.

"At home the tributes at the meeting of the Bar and the funeral services, both in December, 1858, were of a remarkable character, both as to the speakers and the words they spoke. Mr. Justice Nelson of the Supreme Court of the United States, long our ideal in bearing, manner and every element of judicial fitness, presided at the meeting of the Bar. Samuel J. Tilden, conspicuous then and always for his clear insight and great professional and political sagacity; Judge Kent, a man of rare accomplishments and the finest sympathies; Marshall S. Bidwell, a jurist affluent in learning and of high Christian character; Judge Edmonds, noted for his fearlessness in the discharge of duty, and his enthusiasm in every cause he deemed a righteous one; Daniel Lord, the type and fit exemplar of the commercial lawyer in the highest sense, a representative of all that was best in the great metropolis of the Nation, united in terms of eulogy which would seem extravagant and overcolored if their truth were not attested by the strong, unmistakable personal emotion which marked their utterances."

Judge William Kent referred to my grandfather, after his removal from Washington to New York, at only forty years of age, as having become *primus inter pares* with the skilled veterans of the metropolitan Bar. Continuing with the tribute to his professional character, he said:

"On one feature I love to linger; I allude to his treatment of his junior associates. He encouraged the young lawyer

35

in his timid efforts, and unrestrainedly presented all he knew to the compeer counsel who was associated with him."

"He was a man," said Doctor Bethune, "in whose piety was his life."

If praise from Sir Hubert is praise indeed, what can be said of praise from such men as Judge Kent and the others who paid these tributes to my grandfather's memory. My father concludes his review of his father's life as follows:

"Few men were ever more fully and constantly occupied in weighty matters of private and public concern, or more keenly sensitive to the responsibilities they imposed. . . . His rare liberality and catholicity of spirit and the regard for the rights of all men, religious, social and political, which he carried into practice with a rare consistency and consideration, kept him singularly free from personal asperities even in the heated party conflicts in which he sometimes found himself opposed to friends and associates; and he harbored no resentments against men who had done him cruel and malicious wrong.

"He was deeply and sincerely religious; a rare specimen of true piety without a trace of bigotry or even of sectarianism, for he was as catholic in his faith as he was humane in his sympathies. I cannot exaggerate or overstate my sense of his virtues, which were the fruit and flower of divine grace working in a nature which seemed responsive to its heavenly touch to a degree seldom seen in the sons of men.

"His grave is at Woodlawn Cemetery, and on the stone which marks it are carved, according to his direction, beside the Scripture text which attests his Christian faith and trust, and a record of his services in the Cabinets of Jackson and Van Buren, these words, commemorative of his share in the greatest work of his life:

"A Commissioner To Revise The Statute Laws Of The State Of New York."

Chapter III

MY FATHER AND HIS RELATIONS
TO THE SUPREME COURT

MY FATHER, William Allen Butler, and my mother, Mary Russell Marshall, daughter of Captain Charles Henry Marshall of the Black Ball Line of Packet Ships, were married on March 21, 1850 in New York City. Their honeymoon in Washington was the beginning of a married life of unbroken happiness for over fifty years. They celebrated their Golden Wedding in 1900 at the family home, Round Oak, Yonkers.

At my grandfather's request Reverdy Johnson of Maryland, then Attorney General of the United States, moved the admission to the Bar of the Supreme Court of the United States of my father on April 4, 1850. My father was then twenty-five years of age. Mother used to say that the two great events while they were in Washington were father's admission to the Bar of the Supreme Court, and the funeral services for John C. Calhoun, which took place in the Senate Chamber and for which they had front gallery seats.

Father did not make his first appearance before the Supreme Court until some years later, but from that time until his death in 1902 he argued many important cases before it. Some of them were determinative of novel questions of admiralty and maritime law. In the majority of them the Court upheld the principles for which he contended.

His relations with the Court as a body and with the members of the Bench socially were most pleasant. In one case, though he was not successful, while he was contending against overwhelming odds, Chief Justice Waite wrote to

37

one of my sisters that her father's presentation of the case—which was an exceedingly complicated one—was the ablest statement of facts he had ever heard.* This compliment will be appreciated by my lawyer readers who know the difficulties connected with making such statements. Nevertheless my father once remarked that while it was very gratifying to have received such a compliment from the Court, which later delivered an adverse opinion, the pleasure of the compliment was hardly equal to the disappointment occasioned by the opinion.

Mr. Alvin Johnson, who until his untimely death in an accident, was the very able Editor-in-Chief of "The Dictionary of American Biography," once told me that no member of the family of anyone whose memory was to be perpetuated by that publication, would be allowed to write that person's biography. The *raison d'être* for this rule seemed to be based on the idea that it would prevent undue eulogy. Perhaps Mr. Johnson was right. On the other hand, it is possible more accurate information might be obtained from a member of the family than from a stranger.

However most of the material for the truthful but rather eulogistic biography of my father in the Dictionary is credited to a Memorial written by his friend and my one-time partner, Judge George C. Holt, with my assistance, and to his own "Retrospect," both of which were family productions.

The following account of my father's relations with the Supreme Court and of other incidents in his life is a combination of Mr. Johnson's ideas and my own as to how the task of producing such a memorial could best be accomplished.

After my father's death on September 9, 1902, the Memorial Committee of the Bar Association of the City of New York consulted my brother, William Allen Butler, Jr., and myself as to who should prepare the material for the Memorial Book of the Association. All the family united in asking

* (Hoyt v. Sprague 103 U.S. 613.)

Mr. George C. Holt to prepare the memorial. Mr. Holt had known my father for many years and had been the senior partner of my own firm of Holt & Butler for nearly ten years. Later he became District Judge of the United States for the Southern District of New York.

Mr. Holt consented to prepare the Memorial provided the factual material was furnished by our family. My particular duty was to supply the titles of cases argued by my father in the New York Court of Appeals and the Supreme Court of the United States.

The Memorial written by George Holt was read—an unusual and highly complimentary proceeding—at a meeting of the Bar Association. Judge Holt was then about sixty years of age. More than thirty years later, when he passed away at over ninety years of age, his family asked me to write the record of his life for the Memorial Book of the Bar Association.

In as much as part of Judge Holt's Memorial was obtained from data furnished by me, there seems to be no reason why it should not be practically, although not literally, transplanted into this review of my father's legal activities without my being charged with plagiarism. What follows, therefore, can to a large extent be regarded, even when not included within quotation marks, as the result of the joint work of Judge Holt and myself. The Memorial tells of my father's birth at Albany, New York, February 20, 1825; of his going to Washington with his father when the latter became Attorney General; of the warm friendship between Martin Van Buren and my father which began during his boyhood and continued until the death of Mr. Van Buren; of the return of the Butler family to New York; of his college life at the University of the City of New York, from which he was graduated in the Class of 1843, and of his devotion not only to his Class but to his Alma Mater, on the Council of which he served for many years, during part of which time he was its President; of his delivery of a course of lectures on Admiralty Law in the Law School of the University, which was established by his own father, and of other incidents in his long and active life.

After referring to Father's admission to the State Bar in 1846 and to the various firms with which he was connected, and to the fact that his father-in-law, Captain Charles H. Marshall, was on the New York Board of Pilot Commissioners from 1845 to 1865, for which Board Father became counsel at an early age, the Memorial proceeds:

"Although Congress has power to regulate pilotage for the Ports of the United States, including that of New York, it had usually been left under control of the States. A vicious system of political control in the creation and maintenance of the New York Board of Port Wardens, which resulted in terrible disasters on Rockaway Beach and the shipwreck of the vessels the *Bristol* and the *Mexico,* with the loss of many lives, in the years 1836 and 1837, excited a storm of public indignation, and the Port Warden system was abolished. In 1845 the State [of New York] repealed all its pilotage laws, apparently expecting that the matter would be adequately regulated by Congress; but it was not. The Chamber of Commerce and the Board of Marine Underwriters thereupon formed a voluntary association for the licensing and government of pilots, which continued until 1853, when the Legislature passed an act creating a Board of Commissioners of Pilots, on the basis of the existing voluntary organization, providing that three commissioners should be elected by the Chamber of Commerce and two by the Board of Marine Underwriters.

"The constitutionality of this act was questioned on the ground that the method of the appointment of the commissioners by non-political organizations was contrary to the Constitution of the State and also on the fundamental ground that Congress alone had authority to pass laws regulating the subject of pilotage." In the legal battles that followed, "Mr. Butler successfully maintained the constitutionality of the law, which has remained in force ever since [1903]. It is believed that the Pilotage Board affords the sole instance in the State of New York of public officers appointed by private organizations having no political or public authority. It is a matter of public congratulation that a method should have been selected for the appointment of this board having in charge such important interests in connection with the commerce of this port, which has always kept it free from political influences, and Mr. Butler is entitled to much of the credit for the establishment and maintenance of the system.

"Besides the regulation of pilotage the board was empowered by the Legislature to prevent encroachments on the public piers, . . ." which was also fought in the Courts but "Mr. Butler succeeded in setting aside a grant made by the Common Council of a pier in the North River and compelled the proprietors of private steamship lines to desist from the exclusive possession of piers to the injury of general commerce. This led to legislation establishing the present [1903] system permitting the erection of sheds on certain piers for the exclusive use of vessels employed in regular lines and the setting aside of other piers for the general use of commerce.

"Mr. Butler's position as counsel for the Board of Pilot Commissioners naturally led to his being frequently retained in general admiralty business. He was engaged in a large number of the most important admiralty cases brought in his time in New York . . ." and which reached the highest court. In one of these he established "the rule in collision cases that if either vessel has violated an express provision of a statute establishing a rule of navigation, the burden of proof is upon her to establish that such violation could not have contributed in any way to the disaster . . ."; in another his contention was upheld "that materialmen furnishing supplies to a vessel in her home port acquired no lien by general maritime law as adopted by the United States,

41

but that the States, until Congress acts, can authorize such liens by statutes, and that such statutes, although not capable of enforcement by proceedings *in rem* in the State courts, can be enforced in the United States Courts; . . . again that a New York contract of affreightment to ship goods by an English steamer to an English port where the freight was to be paid in English currency, was an American contract, so that a stipulation exempting the carrier from responsibility for the negligence of its servants was void under the rule established by the United States Supreme Court in regard to land transportation although by the law of the State of New York, of England, and the general maritime law existing upon the Continent of Europe such stipulations for exemption are valid.

"But Mr. Butler's professional labor was not at all confined to Admiralty Law. . . . No man at the New York Bar in his time had a more diversified and general practice as a reference to some of the leading cases in which he was engaged, outside of Admiralty, will show."

After referring to several very important cases argued in the New York Court of Appeals where my father constantly appeared, the Memorial mentions cases argued in the Supreme Court of the United States, in one of which, a large loan was held to have been made to a corporation, although the bond to secure it was the individual bond of its president; another, already alluded to was a case of extraordinary complexity, in which an unsuccessful attempt was made to hold the estate of a guardian for investments of his ward's property made many years before in the stock of a manufacturing corporation.

From this point on the Memorial was written by Judge Holt himself who relates:

"These cases and others which might be cited, in which Mr. Butler was the leading counsel, generally involved very large amounts and very important legal questions, and it is at once apparent from a consideration of the general class of questions involved how wide was the scope of his professional practice. His general rank as a lawyer was very high. As a consulting counsel, supervising the extensive work of a very large office, his advice was judicious and accurate; as an advocate he was admirable, both in the trial of cause in courts of first instance and upon appeals. His legal learning was great. He was the master of a style of marked distinction, lucidity and force.

"A peculiarly charming feature of his advocacy was the wit with which he almost always enlivened his arguments. His humor was always kindly and natural. It was never too prominent, but almost always, in any argument that he made, there were touches of bright and spontaneous humor here and there, which admirably illustrated his argument and always added a charm to it. His wit was never sarcastic and never wounded. He was especially courteous to young lawyers whom he met at the Bar. Many letters were written to members of his family after his death, in which grateful references were made to this trait in his character.

"It is almost impossible to do justice to such a light and evanescent thing as humor in specifying instances of it, so much depends on the circumstances and the individuality of the man who is the author of it; but I venture to give a few instances of Mr. Butler's humor, well knowing how inadequate any such instances may be.

"He was at one time opening a case to the jury growing out of the failure of a merchant who had been engaged in the East India trade, and whose failure was caused by the fall in price of a large quantity of manila hemp he had ordered. Mr. Butler, after stating the facts, said that this firm, like certain other unfortunate persons, was finally suspended by too much hemp.

Again, on one occasion "I heard him begin the argument of an appeal in this way: 'May it please the Court. This action was begun about thirty years ago; the original plaintiff is dead, the substituted plaintiff is dead; the original defendant is dead; all of the counsel originally connected with the case are dead; and the principal question upon this appeal is whether the cause of action survives.'

"Mr. Butler was particularly accurate in his knowledge of the Bible. It was very dangerous for anyone in his presence to make a misquotation from that source. He was once attending a church meeting in which a project was on foot for raising money, and someone made a speech in which he urged with much insistence the example of the widow's mite in the Bible. When he finished Mr. Butler arose and stated that he regretted to be obliged to correct the preceding speaker, but that the Bible contained nothing about a widow's mite; a statement which was received with exclamations of surprise and incredulity by the entire audience. They were subdued however when Mr. Butler added: 'The widow spoken of in the Bible contributed *two* mites to the object to which her charity was directed, an example which should not be overlooked by those intending to make small contributions to this cause. (It might be added that the entire amount required was raised, the gentleman who had brought forward his 'Widow's Mite' doubling his own subscription.)

"A motion once made by Mr. Butler to have a person brought in as a party in a rather late stage of the proceeding, the result of which would be to enable him to share with others in the distribution of a fund, was strongly opposed, the counsel repeatedly asserting that the party was applying to come in at the 'eleventh hour.' All that Mr. Butler said in reply was that if the Court would consult the authority referred to by his learned opponent it would find that the man who came in at the eleventh hour got as much as all the rest. His motion was granted.

"But it was as a literary man that Mr. Butler was most widely known by the general public. When a very young man he achieved an extraordinary sucess in literature by the poem called 'Nothing To Wear.'

44

"This poem he first published anonymously. It immediately obtained great popularity in this country and in England, was translated into several languages, and achieved that supreme test of excellence of having its authorship claimed by one of those strange creatures who frequently attempt to obtain the credit of anonymous publications.

" 'Nothing To Wear' was so well known that it was often jokingly referred to in Mr. Butler's presence, and whenever such a reference was made in the midst of any serious business the effect on him was very disconcerting. He was once trying a case against Mr. Bourke Cockran in which it was necessary to prove the value of a stock which contained, among other things, fifty dozen fichus. 'Won't you explain to the jury,' said Mr. Butler, 'what a fichu is?'

"Mr. Cockran broke in with:

" 'That's not necessary, Mr. Butler. Everybody knows that a fichu is an article that a lady puts on when she has *Nothing to Wear.*'

"It was some time before Mr. Butler could bring the Court and the jury back to serious consideration of the case."

To return to the memorial address of Judge Holt, from which I have already quoted at some length:

"Mr. Butler was a Republican in politics all his life, and at almost every Presidential election he made a speech in Yonkers on the political issues of the election. These speeches were usually published. They were characterized by a distinction of style and a nobility of thought which gave them rank among the finest political addresses of his time. He never filled any political or judicial office, and it is a subject of sincere regret that a man so highly qualified to render valuable service in such capacities should have been left, through a long life in this State, without being called into the public service."

The conclusion of the memorial address, of which Judge Holt was the sole author, and which expressed his own appreciation of my father's character as well as that of many of his contemporaries, reads as follows:

"It is natural, in the memorials of members of this association, to err on the side of eulogy. But Mr. Butler's life and character were so praiseworthy that it is difficult to speak of them with due reserve. He was a perfect gentleman. His clear-cut intellectual face, like a Greek cameo, and his whole bearing always gave the impression both of power and distinction. He was a man of wide cultivation and of taste for all graceful and beautiful things. He had an unusually affectionate and domestic nature. He was very fond of his family, his relations, his friends, his home, his books.

"Even the bitter trial which befell him in the last few years of his life, in the loss of his eyesight, did not affect the unvarying serenity, and the sweetness of his character. He had, without ostentation, a deeply reverent and devotional nature. This is particularly shown in his serious poetry, which is almost always tinged with a deep religious feeling. In short, in all the relations of life, he was a man entitled to the highest admiration.

"In estimating his actual rank as a lawyer and a literary man it may probably be admitted that there were a few lawyers of his time of greater eminence, and a few literary men of his time of greater reputation, but I think it is an entirely accurate statement to assert that no man of his time, either in England or America, held an equally high rank, both as a lawyer and a literary man."

Alluding once again to the poem "Nothing To Wear," it was not the only practical product of my father's pen. Attention may be called to lines that met the light of day in *Harper's Monthly*, which are entitled "General Average." In these lines he tells the story of an attempt by a dishonest shipper to profit from a disaster in which his goods were salvaged and subject to the average adjustment, instead, as he claimed, of having been lost and thus entitling him to be paid therefor. There is really no better legal definition of General Average than in these lines:

> "Some things we all dread, and not the least among these
> The dangers and perils and risks of the seas;
> Since the hour Sinbad first scared slumber away,
> To the last Marine list just published today,
> Insatiable Ocean has ceased not to vex
> Our lives with his storms and disasters and wrecks.
> As truly this moment as when Horace penned
> His ode to his outbound, sea-going friend,
> All voyages are ventures, each good ship that sails
> The toy of the tempest, the sport of the gales;
> Still Africus, Eurus and Notus will blow
> Through the cleft thunder cloud, or whirlwind of snow.
> Round ancient Charybdis the breakers still roar,
> And wave chases wave to some wreck-sprinkled shore.
> Thus, circled with perils, ship, cargo and freight,
> Involved in one common adventure and fate,
> When disaster befalls, 'tis equal and fair
> That all the full burden should bear,
> Each paying its just and proportionate share,
> Which joint contribution, on this equal scale,
> Is called 'General Average,' whence hangs our tale."

CHAPTER IV

THE *SCOTLAND* CASE

PURPOSELY OMITTED from the list of cases referred to in Judge Holt's memorial address, were two cases argued by my father in the Supreme Court of the United States. They were the *Scotland* Case * and the *Juilliard* vs. *Greenman* Case.† Each of them deserves special mention. They are landmarks in our legal history.

Few people, leaving or entering New York Harbor, who pass the Scotland Lightship, have any idea why that vessel is so named. Still fewer are alive who have personal knowledge of the cause that gave the name to that beacon of safety for millions of people on their voyages to and from one of the greatest commercial ports of the world.

The opening paragraph of Justice Bradley's opinion of the Supreme Court of the United States, as reported in the Case of the *Scotland*, tells the story that gave name to the lightship. The steamship *Scotland*, of the National Steam Navigation Company, a British corporation, sailed from New York for Liverpool on December 1, 1866. After reaching the high seas off Fire Island Light it collided with an American ship, *Kate Dyer*, bound from Callao, Peru, to New York, and laden with a cargo of guano, the property of the Government of Peru. The *Kate Dyer* sank immediately with a total loss of ship and cargo.

The *Scotland*, suffering severely from the collision, turned back; but before reaching Sandy Hook she also sank—a total

* (105 U.S. 24.)
† (110 U.S. 421.)

48

THE SUPREME COURT OF THE UNITED STATES
1890

(Centennial Picture)

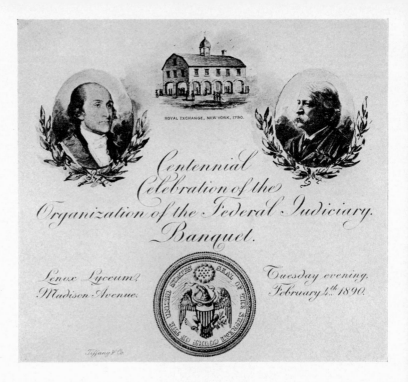

FRONT COVER AND SECOND PAGE OF SOUVENIR MENU
AND PROGRAM CENTENNIAL CELEBRATION BANQUET

loss except for a small amount of wreckage, consisting of anchors, chains and rigging, worth about $2,500.

The Coast Guard immediately set a buoy to mark the spot where the *Scotland* had sunk because its wreck was a menace to navigation. Shortly thereafter the United States Government installed, and has ever since maintained, the lightships which have always marked the spot and borne the name of the ill-fated *Scotland*.

The court opinion referred to was delivered in a case brought by the owners of the *Kate Dyer* and of her cargo to recover damages for their loss from the owners of the *Scotland*. The case had been tried and decided in favor of the claimants in the District Court in which the owners of the *Scotland* were represented by an admiralty lawyer who, before the case was reached on appeal, had been elevated to the Bench and had turned this case and others over to my father's firm. On appeal the Circuit Court also decided the case against the owners of the *Scotland*. Appeal was taken to the Supreme Court of the United States.

There were two angles to the case: one was the question of liability for the collision; and the other was whether or not the owners of the *Scotland* as a foreign corporation, could limit their liability to the value of the vessel after the collision, under the Limited Liability Act of 1851.

Both lower courts had ruled against the owner of the *Scotland* on both points. The case was argued in the Supreme Court of the United States in April 1881, and was held without decision until March 1882 when the Court handed down its decision sustaining both courts below as far as responsibility for the collision was concerned. It reversed them both, however, on the issue of limitation of liability.

As this was the principal question involved, the decision was a victory for Father, who had personally argued the case, and for his colleagues—his partner, Thomas E. Stillman, and John Chetwood.

The owners of the *Kate Dyer* were represented by James C. Carter, one of the most eminent members of the New York Bar, and Robert D. Benedict, one of the leaders of the Admiralty Bar. The Peruvian Government, owner of the cargo, was represented by Joseph H. Choate.

When the decision of the United States Supreme Court was announced the total amount of the possible liability of the owners of the *Scotland*, with interest, was about $500,000. In anticipation of an adverse judgment, the owners, during the fifteen years the suit had been pending, had accumulated a sinking fund for that sum, which was released by the decision and used for the building of a new steamship to add to the National Steam Navigation Company operating between New York and Liverpool.

Not long before the United States Supreme Court rendered its decision, the owners of the *Scotland*, being greatly worried by the delay of the Court in announcing it, made a very substantial offer of settlement. The offer was refused and shortly thereafter the decision was given out. This was a great blow to Mr. Benedict, a man much older than myself, but a dear friend, who, in my opinion, never recovered from the shock and disappointment caused by the decision.

The seriousness of the questions involved was demonstrated by the fact that the Supreme Court would not decree costs to either party as against the other, saying that the question of limitation of liability "was a new one upon which there was wide difference of opinion; and neither Court nor parties had any precedents to guide or direct them as to the mode of proceeding."

Credit must be given, therefore, to Father and his colleagues for having convinced the Supreme Court of the justice of their client's cause without prior decisions of the courts to support their arguments, which thus rested on the elementary rules of law and justice. According to some these rules do not always coincide.

It is said that as Justice Holmes was leaving the banquet

hall after the farewell dinner tendered him by the Boston Bar, before he left for Washington to take his seat on the Bench of the Supreme Court of the United States, someone called out:

"Now justice will be administered in Washington."

To this the new justice is reported to have replied:

"Don't be too sure. I am going there to administer *the law.*"

This perhaps was exemplified by his decision in the case of Blackstone vs. Miller, which is referred to in a later chapter of this book.

In connection with the case of the *Scotland* a rather amusing incident occurred. It was the only occasion on which anybody ever spoke, in my hearing, of my father as a "damned fool." There was the usual consultation among members of his firm as to the charges for this very successful victory. Their client, of course, was prepared to recompense them substantially for their valuable services. The amount of the charges was still to be determined. One of the partners, coming out of the conference, said to another partner, who had just entered the office:

"That man Butler is a damned fool."

In response to a question as to the reason for this extraordinary statement, the partner who had made it explained:

"He only wants to charge so much in the *Scotland* Case and the rest of us think that it ought to be more than twice that amount."

In the end, however, a very substantial charge was agreed upon, which was cheerfully paid by the client. Thus it was shown that Father was not quite as devoid of sense as one of his partners seemed to think he was.

Any of my readers who henceforth pass the Scotland Lightship will not only know why it is so called, but can tell the story to fellow passengers who may be unaware of the origin of its name.

Chapter V

THE CASE OF JUILLIARD VS. GREENMAN

FATHER USED to tell of a conversation which took place in the House of Representatives during the consideration of a bill which became the Act of May 31, 1878. This Act provided for the re-issuance, for governmental purposes, of United States Notes—then known as Greenbacks—which had been redeemed in gold after the resumption of specie payment.

General Benjamin F. Butler, who bore the same name as my grandfather but, so far as can be ascertained, was not related to our family, was then a member of Congress from Massachusetts, and sponsored the bill. Mr. Simeon B. Chittenden, a member of Congress from New York, opposed it. They were the ones who held the conversation of which my father told. Mr. Chittenden said to General Butler:

"If this bill becomes a law, the Supreme Court of the United States will hold it to be unconstitutional:"

The General retorted:

"I'll bet you $5,000 that the Court will sustain it and I'll argue any case that comes up myself."

Mr. Chittenden was not a lawyer, but was a client and a great admirer of my father. He declined to accept the bet. He told General Butler, however, that if the constitutionality of the law could be tested in the Supreme Court of the United States, he would engage counsel to represent the party alleging its unconstitutionality, adding that it would probably cost him more than the amount of the bet to do so.

After Congress adjourned Mr. Chittenden retained my father not only to argue such a case but also to assist him in having such a case created, in order that the constitutional question involved therein might be tested.

Under the then existing law, to reach the Supreme Court of the United States, such a case must comprise a *bona fide* cause of action involving more than $5,000. So some party must be found willing to refuse the offer of payment of a legal debt of more than $5,000 in Greenbacks, which had been redeemed in gold and then re-issued by the Government under the Act of 1878. The creditor was obliged to take the risk of losing his debt in case the Court decided the tender was good, as he would then have no right to recover it in any other action.

It was necessary also that the suit should be between citizens of different States so that the federal courts could obtain jurisdiction of the case under the diverse citizenship provisions of the Constitution. Under such circumstances— if the sum involved was more than $5,000—the defeated party would have the right to appeal directly to the Supreme Court of the United States.

Mr. Augustus D. Juilliard, a wholesale dealer in textile goods, was a client of my father's office. He was a man of ample means, a resident of New York City and an advocate of "hard money." He became interested in the case and offered to take the risk involved. Mr. Juilliard was a public spirited citizen and a frequent and generous contributor to enterprises for civic relief. He was the founder of the Juilliard Musical Foundation in New York City.

In the regular course of business Juilliard sold merchandise—costing $5,122.90—to Mr. Greenman in Mystic, Connecticut, where Greenman lived and carried on business.

At the Sub-Treasury in New York City—this happened before the establishment of the Federal Reserve Bank system—Greenman's representative offered two legal tender notes, which were known as United States Greenbacks. One was for $5,000 and the other for $100. He asked for gold in payment for them. Having received the gold he took

53

it to another window of the Sub-Treasury and asked for legal tender notes in exchange for the gold.

At this other window he received the same bills he had previously asked to have redeemed in gold. The numbers and exact description of these bills had, of course, been carefully noted by at least two witnesses.

Through this procedure these particular Greenbacks had actually been redeemed and had actually been re-issued under the provisions of the Act of 1878. The details of the above narrated transactions at the Sub-Treasury do not appear in the statement of the case as reported. They are the actual facts of the case, however, so far as the redemption and re-issuance of the United States notes are concerned. They are stated of my own knowledge because the transaction occurred during my connection with my father's office.

There is nothing in the history of the case to show whether re-issuance of the Greenbacks, immediately given back for the gold which had just been received in redemption of the same notes, was by prearrangement, or was what my father used to describe as a "first-class coincidence." Anyhow the evidence in the case showed they were the same notes.

The next move of Greenman was to tender to Juilliard, in payment of his indebtedness, those two bills, with twenty-two dollars and ninety cents in gold and other legal tender. Juilliard refused to accept the tender, except for the twenty-two dollars and ninety cents in coin. Juilliard gave as his reason for such action that, as the particular Greenbacks tendered him had been redeemed and paid, they could not again be issued as legal tender notwithstanding that an Act of Congress might so provide. Greenman declined to make payment in any other manner. Greenman claimed that as his tender had been in legal tender money of the United States, he was under no further obligations in regard thereto.

Then Juilliard sued Greenman in the Supreme Court of the State of New York for the balance of the account.

54

Greenman, as a citizen of Connecticut, availed himself of the provision of the Judiciary Act to transfer the case, on the ground of diverse citizenship, to the Circuit Court of the United States for the Southern District of New York. There the case was tried and decided against Juilliard. As more than $5,000 was involved, Juilliard appealed the case to the Supreme Court of the United States.* In that Court it was argued by George F. Edmunds, a foremost leader of the Bar, at that time United States Senator from Vermont, and my father. They both maintained that the Act of 1878 was unconstitutional and that the tender made by Greenman was not good.

General Ben Butler—as he was usually called—Thomas H. Talbot of Massachusetts and James McKeen of New York argued the case in support of the constitutionality of the Act and the legality of the tender, and won a signal victory over their distinguished and able opponents.

Mr. Justice Gray wrote the opinion which practically sustained the right of the United States as a sovereign state to issue money and to make its notes legal tender in payment of private debts in time of peace as well as in time of war. A strong dissent was written by Mr. Justice Field in which, however, none of the other justices concurred.

Without in any way claiming to be a good prophet, especially as to how the Supreme Court of the United States may decide the cases submitted to it, this decision did not at all surprise me. Yet it did involve disappointment because of my father's connection with the case. When this decision was rendered there was a strong trend in the Court toward the national sovereignty of the Government of the United States in all matters relating to the country as a whole—a doctrine of which I am an ardent disciple.

There was some comment as to whether Juilliard vs. Greenman was really a *bona fide* case. It is competent for me, from my personal knowledge of the facts involved, to

* (Juilliard v. Greenman, 110 U.S. 421.)

state that it was. The transactions alleged actually took place, including the sale, tender, redemption and re-issuance of the notes, and refusal to accept. Whether or not these events were made in order to create an issue for the courts to decide, the case was not moot, but a real and justifiable one.

Some years after this case had been decided, General Ben Butler and I, between whom a pleasant acquaintance had grown, met at Halifax, Nova Scotia, in the lobby of the Halifax Hotel. He invited me to go as far as Boston on his yacht, which was then in Halifax Harbor. This yacht was the world-famous *America,* which won the Queen's Cup in 1851 by sailing around the Isle of Wight and outsailing all her competitors. When Queen Victoria asked which yacht was the winner she was told that the Yankee was the winner. And when she asked which yacht was second, the reply she received was: "There was no second, Your Majesty."

The *America* was disposed of by her owners, who had sailed her to that international victory which has never been overcome, notwithstanding the efforts of Lord Dunraven, Sir Thomas Lipton and other English yachtsmen. During the Civil War she was used by the United States Navy and was sunk. General Butler bought, raised and converted the *America* into a private yacht for his personal use.

On expressing my regret that his invitation to sail to Boston with him could not be accepted, he changed it to one for breakfast 'on board' the next morning. This invitation was cheerfully accepted. The General's gig—this was before the days of electric, or even naphtha launches—awaited me at the wharf and took me to his yacht. He met me at the head of the gangway, escorted me to the dining room and said:

"Now, Butler, your grandfather had the same name as mine, and he and your father were both lawyers, and perhaps better lawyers than I am. I know they were better Christians, but I am sure neither of them was as good a judge of Medford rum as I am,—so let's have some."

For the first and only time my breakfast started with a jorum of Medford rum, or for that matter of any kind of rum. My experience with that particular beverage does not permit me to express an opinion as to whether it was any better than any other brand of that ilk, but it certainly was good.

This was the last time it was my pleasure to see the General, but the breakfast we had on the *America* in Halifax Harbor will always be among my pleasantest memories. The General had often been in my father's office during the progress of the Juilliard vs Greenman Case and we had become very pleasantly acquainted. So whenever the Juilliard Case is referred to, the disappointment caused by the decision therein is greatly mitigated by the remembrance of our breakfast on the *America* and that jorum of Medford Rum with which the General and I began it.

Chapter VI

AFTER MY FATHER'S DEATH

JUDGE HOLT'S Memorial Address was not the only one presented in appropriate proceedings after my father's death. Mr. John E. Parsons, one of the most prominent members of the New York Bar, who as my father had been, also at one time was President of the New York City Bar Association, presented a Memorial Address to the Appellate Division of the First Department of the New York Supreme Court. With reference to Father's long and active professional career, Mr. Parsons said:

"Mr. Butler began the practice of the law with the advantage and the peril of a professional association with a great lawyer—his father, whose name and fame as a lawyer and as an advocate, still are, and long will be, remembered. If such a reputation is inheritable, it is a burden or a benefit to the heir, according to his capacity to administer the succession. Mr. Butler's career at this Bar may be summed up by the statement that his death left it undiminished."

After reviewing a number of events and incidents of my father's civil and professional career, Mr. Parsons closed his address with these words:

"Mr. Butler's life, and that of his distinguished father, cover a period which connects the present with the far different kind of professional life and work in the early years of the past century. During the many years which he devoted to his profession he was a marked figure. It is no disparagement of others to say that from the beginning his position was in the very front rank.

"Following upon the renown, which by his name he inher-

58

ited, his position might in a special sense be described as unique. The members of his profession have thought that in his case it was exceptionally suitable that there should be inscribed on the records of the Court some reference to his career, and the due expression of regret, when at last, full of years and honor, he passed away."

Presiding Justice Charles H. Van Brunt, who for many years had been a friend and admirer of my father, responded to the Memorial Address of Mr. Parsons and directed that it be inscribed upon the minutes of the Court. Justice Van Brunt spoke of the deep regret felt by the Court over the death of Mr. Butler, "who was one of the few remaining links which connect the past with the present and the old with the new." He alluded to the accurate method pursued by my father in his statement of facts in opening his cases, which has already been mentioned as an art of which he was a past master. Justice Van Brunt then said:

"There was one feature in his presentation of his cases to the Court which always struck me as being exceedingly remarkable, and I know of no one who excelled him in that regard and few that equalled him. He evidently had prepared his cases with great care, had studied them in all the lights to which they were subject, and he was enabled to state all the facts of the case clearly, accurately and with precision, being careful not to leave out those which might tend against the view which he desired to enforce upon the Court. So that when he had gotten through with his statement of the case, the Court might feel confident that they were possessed of all the facts which were necessary to apply the principles which he would then seek to lay before the Court. I regret to say that our experience of today shows that his example has been rarely followed in that particular."

Father's memory was also appropriately recognized by the Bar of the District Court of the United States for the Southern District of New York, where his frequent appearances had made him an outstanding figure of the Admiralty

Bar. Here the Memorial Address was presented by Robert D. Benedict, Father's leading opponent in the Case of the *Scotland,* which has been fully related in Chapter IV. Mr. Benedict magnanimously referred to the fame Father had won by that case, which, by the same token, was one of Mr. Benedict's most disappointing defeats. Mr. Benedict concluded his address as follows:

"Mr. Butler's clear conception of principles, his acute and powerful reasoning, and, above all, his fairness and courtesy as an advocate, will always entitle him to a high place among the great lawyers of the Admiralty, and to the pleasantest of memories among his fellows of the Admiralty Bar."

In 1911, nearly ten years after Father's death, my mother presented to the Court of Appeals of the State of New York a portrait of him which was painted by my brother, Howard Russell Butler. It hangs in the lobby entrance to the Court Room in the Capitol at Albany. In the fire in the Capitol already referred to as having practically destroyed the Law Library, as well as many works of art in the building, this portrait escaped destruction.

The presentation was made on Mother's behalf by the Honorable Alton B. Parker, formerly the Chief Justice of the Court. Opening his address by describing the portrait, Judge Parker said:

"Skill and love have wrought so wonderfully well that from this canvas William Allen Butler, his very self, seems to look out upon us with the old dignity and kindliness. The portrait is indeed faithfully true to the original. 'The end has crowned the work; the high endeavor and the long toil with full success are blest.'"

Chief Justice Edgar M. Cullen, in expressing the pleasure of the Court at receiving the portrait and the Court's thanks to the donor, said:

"William Allen Butler, whose likeness is now before us, was a gentleman of great culture and refinement, a ripe scholar, and possessed of literary ability of a high order; but it is his standing as a great lawyer and advocate that renders it appropriate that his portrait should hang on the walls of the entrance to this Court Room, so that members of the profession of coming generations may see how the man, whose distinction and learning they will know only either historically or by tradition, appeared in the flesh, and may be aroused to emulate his character and achievements."

Howard Russell Butler, my brother, painted several other oil portraits of my father. One hangs in the Presidential Gallery of the New York City Bar Association, and another in New York University, of which Father was an alumnus. Also he was later a member of its Council and for a time President of the Council.

Even as the chapter relating to my grandfather closed with the filial tribute of a son, so let me close this chapter with a tribute of filial and affectionate respect for both my father and my grandfather, as expressed nearly forty years ago when my work on the "Treaty Making Power of the United States" was published. These volumes were dedicated to my grandfather, but the preface contains this paragraph:

These volumes have been dedicated to my grandfather, but in order that the name of my father, William Allen Butler, may also in some manner be linked with them, they will make their first appearance on the anniversary of his birth—February 20, 1825—on which he completed the seventy-seventh year of his life.

For more than fifty-five years he has been a member of the New York Bar in active practice; he has been President of the American Bar Association and also of the Association of the Bar of the City of New York. On this day, and under these circumstances, it certainly is justifiable for me to refer to the words uttered on an appropriate occasion by the Honorable Joseph H. Choate just before he left this country to resume those duties as our Ambassador at the Court of St. James, which he is so gracefully and efficiently performing. . . . Mr. Choate described my father as "the very dean of our profession and entitled to be so called not only by reason of his seniority, but also from his character, and the manner in which, during his more than half century of practice, he has constantly upheld the honor and dignity of the bar."

For several years before his death my father was practically blind, but his remarkable memory enabled him to do many things that he could not otherwise have accomplished. Few people attending the last New Year's Day services at which he presided in our church at Yonkers, knew that, while apparently reading from the open Bible in his hands, he was repeating from memory the XC and the XCI Psalms. On another occasion, having been reminded of an incident relating to a poem written fifty years previously, he repeated the poem at length, although he had not seen or heard it for many years.

Another feat of memory he revealed was in the preparation of his arguments in the Appellate Court. He would have the record read to him and the reader would mark with blue, red or black pencils the items my father wished to refer to. Then, dictating his brief from memory, he would tell the stenographer to cite the marked passages, the color of the pencil marks indicating how he wished to use them to the best advantage of the party on whose behalf he had been retained. Meanwhile one of his assistants would look up the legal precedents bearing *pro* and *con* on the case. After they had been read to my father he would cite them accordingly. The argument of the case, including citations of authorities, would be entirely from memory.

It was largely on account of his failing eyesight that, during the latter part of his life, my father made many efforts to withdraw from active practice of the law. They were hardly availing, however, because his advice was sought constantly, not only by his clients but also by other attorneys who desired his assistance in difficult legal situations up to the very time of his death.

He devoted all the time he could to his family, participated in church and civic activities, and compiled his reminiscences, which were not edited and published until after his death. When he died the announcement in the press was of the passing of the First Citizen of Yonkers. There was an official display of flags at half-mast in that city although he had not occupied any public office.

His funeral in the First Presbyterian Church of Yonkers, of which he had been a member for many years, was attended by a notable gathering of the prominent citizens of that city, and members of the New York Bar. He was buried in the same plot in Woodlawn Cemetery in which his father had been buried, and where sixteen years afterward, in 1919, were laid the remains of our mother, who had been his faithful and loving helpmate for more than fifty years.

CHAPTER VII

MY REPORTERSHIP IN THE SUPREME
COURT

O N Thursday, December 4, 1902, at the opening of the
Supreme Court of the United States, Chief Justice
Fuller announced that Charles Henry Butler, of New York,
had been appointed Reporter of the Decisions of the Court,
and was charged with the duty of reporting the cases already
decided during the October term which commenced on October 1.* Thereupon the Marshal of the Court escorted me
to the desk of the Clerk of the Court, who administered the
oath of office to me.

Prior to this announcement another oath had been administered to me *in camera,* in the Robing Room of the
Court, of which no official record was kept. This oath was
to the effect that the affiant was a loyal citizen of, and had
never borne arms against the United States, or aided its
enemies in any way.

That oath was, and still is, required of all appointees to
office, as no person who had served in the Army of the
Confederate States could occupy a Federal Office unless he
proved that he had been included in the General Amnesty.
However, it was and is customary to administer this part of
the oath of office *in camera;* and being administered only
to comply with statutory requirements, it is omitted from
the oaths administered publicly.

At the time of my appointment the Court consisted of
Chief Justice Melville Weston Fuller, of Illinois, appointed
by President Cleveland April 30, commissioned July 20,

* (187 U.S.)

MELVILLE W. FULLER

DAVID J. BREWER

JOHN MARSHALL HARLAN

and taking office October 8, 1888; and of the following Associate Justices: John Marshall Harlan, of Kentucky, appointed by President Hayes, commissioned on November 29, 1877, taking office December 10, 1877; David Josiah Brewer, of Kansas, appointed by President Harrison, commissioned December 18, 1889, taking office January 6, 1890; Henry B. Brown, of Michigan, appointed by President Harrison, commissioned December 29, 1890, taking office January 5, 1891; George Shiras, Jr., of Pennsylvania, appointed by President Harrison, commissioned July 26, taking office October 10, 1892; Edward Douglass White, of Louisiana, appointed by President Cleveland, commissioned February 19, and taking office March 13, 1894; (Associate Justice White was later appointed Chief Justice by President Taft on December 12, confirmed the same day, and he took office December 19, 1910, to succeed Chief Justice Fuller); Rufus W. Peckham of New York, appointed by President Cleveland, commissioned December 9, 1895, taking office January 6, 1896; Joseph McKenna of California, appointed by President McKinley, commissioned January 1 and taking office January 6, 1898.

There was one vacancy at the extreme left of the Court. During the previous vacation Justice Horace Gray of Massachusetts—who had been Chief Justice of the Supreme Judicial Court of that State—had died. President Theodore Roosevelt appointed Oliver Wendell Holmes of Massachusetts, who like his predecessor also had been Chief Justice of the Supreme Judicial Court of that State, to fill the vacancy. The nomination of Justice Holmes was confirmed by the Senate, but he did not take his seat until December 8, 1902, four days after the commencement of my term as Reporter.

Justice Holmes continued to be Chief Justice of the Supreme Court of Massachusetts until he was sworn as Associate Justice of the Supreme Court of the United States. As he went onto the Bench he requested me kindly to ask

65

the Marshal to forward a telegram which he handed to me. It was addressed to the Governor of Massachusetts, and in it he resigned his office as Chief Justice of the Supreme Court of that State, with the remark that he could not very well be a justice of two courts at the same time.

And so, taking his seat at the extreme left of the Bench on Monday, December 8, 1902, he gradually worked his way up until he reached the seat on the immediate right of the Chief Justice, having become Senior Justice after the death of Justice McKenna. Here he sat until he retired at the age of nearly ninety-one, January 12, 1932. Justice Van Devanter followed him as Senior Justice of the Court.

For fourteen terms—there was one term each year from October to June—my seat was at the Reporter's desk, just below the extreme left of the Bench. During that period fifty-five volumes of the United States Reports—Nos. 187-241 inclusive—were edited and published. My relations with the members of the Court and its officers were most delightful and congenial. The work was very interesting. It was not difficult and did not take all of my time. The salary and emoluments afforded me a comfortable income. The Reporter, at that time, had the right to sell his volumes to the public at a statutory price, for which privilege the publishers paid a very substantial sum.

Eventually, however, the work became somewhat monotonous. There was nothing constructive about it so far as my part was concerned. When the Court's decisions were referred to unfavorably, as was some times the case—generally by defeated parties—my usual response was a disclaimer of being *particeps criminis* and admitting only being an accessory *after the fact*.

And so one evening in June 1916, upon finishing my work on some opinions to be sent to the printer, I said to my wife:

"What would you think if I resigned the Reportership and returned to active practice?"

66

"Why" she said, "I have been hoping for two years or more that you would do just that."

And that settled it.

Of course the work of the term had to be finished, and it was not until September, 1916 that Chief Justice White was told of my determination to retire. Some years before, this had been suggested to him, but at his instance my intention had been reconsidered. On this occasion he again urged me to remain, but my reply was:

"If the professional steed that is now champing at its bit and neighing outside my door is to be remounted, it must be done before my joints get too stiff."

At his request, however, the actual resignation was withheld until the reconvening of the Court so that the Justices could consider the question of my successor. On October 10, 1916 my resignation was read in open Court. As it was being read, the Marshal handed me a letter signed by all the Justices, which also was read as part of the proceedings of the day. The recipient might indeed be proud of such a letter without being charged with undue conceit; and so it is here reproduced, together with the proceedings of the Court as set forth in the official Reports.

The reading of my resignation and the Court's response thereto were immediately followed by the announcement that my friend, Ernest Knaebel, of Colorado, then Assistant Attorney General of the United States, in charge of land cases had been appointed Reporter in my place. He had argued many cases before the Court during my term of office.

SUPREME COURT OF THE UNITED STATES

Tuesday, October 10, 1916.

Present: The Chief Justice, Mr. Justice McKenna, Mr. Justice Holmes, Mr. Justice Day, Mr. Justice Van Devanter, Mr. Justice Pitney, Mr. Justice McReynolds, Mr. Justice Brandeis, and Mr. Justice Clarke.

The Chief Justice also announced the following order of the court:

It is ordered that the letter of resignation of the Reporter of this court, Charles Henry Butler, Esq., and the response of the court thereto be entered upon the minutes of the court as follows, to wit

Washington, D. C., October 5, 1916.

To the Chief Justice and Associated Justices of the Supreme Court of the United States:

I hereby tender my resignation as Reporter of this court, to take effect on the appointment of my successor.

I cannot do this without thanking you for the kindness and consideration which I have received from all the members of the court during the 14 terms I have had the honor of reporting their decisions.

Very respectfully, your obedient servant,
Chas. Henry Butler.

Supreme Court of the United States,
October 9, 1916.

Dear Sir: In informing you of the acceptance of your resignation, we desire to convey our abiding sense of the courtesy and consideration which you have so uniformly manifested during the many years in which you have been Reporter, and our appreciation of the zealous purpose to discharge fully your duty which has controlled you during that long period.

We can not refrain from hoping that the enlarged field of professional endeavor, the desire to enter upon which has caused you to sever your official relations with the court, may prove as fruitful in good results as you expect it to be, and that you may enjoy a long, happy, and useful life.

Very truly, yours,
Edward D. White.
Joseph McKenna.
Oliver Wendell Holmes.
William R. Day.
Willis Van Devanter.
Mahlon Pitney.
J. C. McReynolds.
Louis D. Brandeis.
John H. Clarke.

Charles Henry Butler, Esq.

And it is further ordered that Mr. Ernest Knaebel, of Colorado, be, and he is hereby, appointed Reporter of this court in the place of Charles Henry Butler, Esq., resigned, and is charged with the duty of reporting the decisions of the present term from its commencement.

Mr. Knaebel's appointment came to him as a surprise. He did not know that the post was vacant. While my resignation was withheld the Court authorized the Chief Justice to tender the office to Mr. Knaebel, which he accepted and has held most satisfactorily for nearly ten years longer than my term.

This was one of the few instances of the office seeking the man instead of the man seeking the office. Since Mr. Knaebel was appointed, the office of Reporter of the Decisions of the Court has been statutorily reorganized.* The Reports are now edited by the Reporter on a salary basis, are printed at the Government Printing Office, and sold by the Superintendent of Documents.

Few understand the nature of the Reporter's office and the functions and duties of its incumbent. More than once letters came to my office asking what system of stenography was used. The word "reporter," as generally understood, does not convey the idea of editing and publishing. The office is an old one and was established under the same name in the English Law Courts centuries ago.

My brother George, as representative of important financial interests, was involved in a law suit that figured largely in the public press. He was constantly annoyed by newspaper reporters. When the announcement was made of my appointment as Reporter of Decisions of the Supreme Court, one of his small sons asked:

"Dad, why does Uncle Harry want that place?"

My brother George answered:

"Because it is a very honorable position."

* (42 Stat. 816.)

"But," his son said, "he can't, of course, come to this house any more."

"Why not?" the father asked.

"Well," replied the son, "I heard you tell John the other day that if another one of those darned reporters rang the bell, to kick him down the front steps and not let him get into the house."

On another occasion, when asked to speak at a club luncheon—not a lawyers' club—my introduction by the presiding officer as the "Head Stenographer of the United States Supreme Court," rather flabbergasted me. After the luncheon, however, my introducer, who meanwhile had been informed by a listener who was a lawyer, that my kind of Reporter was not spelt with a small *r*, was profuse in his apologies. He was told, however, to "forget it," as the luncheon was too good to have the memory of it marred by any mere slip of the tongue.

The Reporter of the Court is appointed by order of the Court. He remains Reporter until the Court appoints someone else in his place. There is no term of office. His appointment is not confirmed by the Senate. Anent this there was a rather amusing incident.

A friend, not a lawyer, but who was well known to our luncheon coterie in the Lawyers' Club of New York, came to the table a few days after my appointment. Referring to it, he said that he was very glad to know that Butler had been confirmed.

"In fact," he told my friends, "I telephoned several Senators and asked them to vote for him."

As his listeners were lawyers, and knew that the Court's appointment needed no confirmation by the Senate, they were more amused than edified by his remarks.

The Justices made no mistake in pre-selecting Mr. Knaebel, nor in keeping my resignation under cover, not only because no better man could have been chosen for the place, but also because the Court avoided the ordeal of making a choice from a crowd of applicants for the post.

After my predecessor, Judge Davis, resigned in 1902 at the opening of the October term, there were more than twenty applicants for the position. The Court did not send for me. The office did not seek me. It was sought by me and fortunately obtained.

Learning of Judge Davis' intention to resign, my name had been suggested by one of my father's partners, General Hubbard, to his life-long friend, fellow citizen of Maine and classmate in college, Chief Justice Fuller, and by others to Justices Harlan, Brown and White. Through the offices of the Banks Law Publishing Company—which published my "Treaty Making Power of the United States" and had also published seventy-seven of the Reports of the Supreme Court Decisions during Judge Davis' tenure of office—full information had been obtained as to the salary and additional emoluments of the office, and this had rather given me the inside track.

For some reason or other the appointment was held up. On December 1, however, Justice Harlan advised me to come to Washington forthwith. We went together to the home of Chief Justice Fuller, who told me to be in the Robing Room of the Court at half-past eleven o'clock. This command was obeyed, of course, with the result that my tenure of office began without further delay.

Speaking of the office seeking the man, and not the man seeking the office, an incident happened at the Metropolitan Club in Washington one evening. There was gathered a group of conversationalists, nearly all of whom, including myself, occupied some kind of Government position. One after another told how he had been sent for, was urged to accept the office offered, and which he finally agreed to accept, much against his will and greatly to his financial disadvantage. When my turn came to speak, the others were somewhat surprised to hear me say something like this:

71

"Well, so far as can be ascertained, you now see before you the one and only man who wanted the position he finally got, by going after it hot-foot and hounding his friends to death to help him get it. Now it seems as though he might better have just sat still and waited for someone to come and make him take the job." This remark broke up the party, and after the next round everybody went home.

The Reporter is an officer of the Court, and, as such, an officer of the United States Government. The Attorney General so held in granting my application for permission to use "penalty envelopes" for my official mail. For eighteen years my predecessor paid postage on all the matter that passed between him and his out-of-town publishers and printers, without knowing, as was ascertained by me in less than twelve days after taking office, that it was entirely unnecessary for him to do so.

The Reporter—as well as the Clerk and the Marshal—attends all the official functions of the Court. For many years, on assembling for its first session of the term, the Court immediately adjourned, as would be solemnly announced by the Chief Justice, "in accordance with immemorial custom to give its members an opportunity of paying their respects to the President of the United States." The Court would proceed then to the White House for a very perfunctory ceremony in the Blue Room.

On one occasion we went down Pennsylvania Avenue two by two, in silk hats and frock coats, and, as was the custom, the Reporter was in the carriage with the Junior Justice, then Mr. Justice Day. As we drove along, the Justice said to me:

"Butler, what a grand thing it would be for the cause of arbitration if the Chief Justice of England [Lord Alverstone] would see the justice of our cause and so make the Alaska award in favor of the United States."

Justice Day, having been Secretary of State when the treaty creating the Alaska Boundary Commission was drawn up, of course was deeply interested in the question. He knew also—as he himself had appointed me—of my connection with the Fairbanks-Herschell Commission of 1898. This commission had attempted unsuccessfully to adjust the Alaska Boundary dispute. The Treaty provided for a decision by four out of the six commissioners. There were three for each country. It was necessary for at least one commissioner to vote against his own country in order to reach an award.

"Yes, indeed, that would be great, Mr. Justice," was my reply. "But suppose Root [who was senior American Commissioner] should see the merits of the other fellow's case, and give the award to Canada—how great would that be for the cause of arbitration?"

"Oh, we can depend on Root!" said Mr. Justice Day.

And so we could, for a few days after this the award was announced in favor of the United States—Lord Alverstone having so voted.

While personally calling on President Theodore Roosevelt some time afterwards, it was impossible to refrain from telling him this story. It amused him greatly and he said:

"Well you know, Butler, Day was right. We surely could depend on Root."

On another occasion we arrived at the White House exactly on the minute of half past twelve o'clock, and were ushered into the Blue Room. President Wilson, who was punctuality itself, immediately entered the room. Greeting Chief Justice White, he walked around the semi-circle, shaking hands with each one of the party. Then turning to the Chief Justice he said:

"You have reconvened for the term?"

"Yes," the Chief Justice replied, "and have adjourned to pay our respects to yourself as President."

"Then, Mr. Chief Justice, I will not detain you longer," said the President, and he went out through the doorway that was just behind him.

73

Exactly five minutes after we had entered the portals of the Executive Mansion, we were on our way out.

Times change. When Mr. Taft became Chief Justice, he directed the Marshal to arrange the appointment with the President for eleven o'clock in the forenoon of the opening day of the Court. Since then the Justices have gathered at the White House and paid their respects to the President before the opening of Court, thus saving an entire day for business. As the Court sits to hear arguments five days in each of fifteen or sixteen weeks, each day represents a large per centum of the entire working term, and so one whole day is a material saving.

During Mr. Taft's term as President, however, things were different. When the Court called at the White House it was entertained by the passing around of liquid refreshment and cigars. About half an hour or so of conversation followed, before the respects of the Court had been fully paid to the Chief Executive.

During my official connection with the United States Supreme Court many amusing incidents occurred.

Once a young lawyer from Kansas argued an appeal in a *habeas corpus* proceeding. His client, who operated a drug store, had been arrested for selling liquor to an "allottee" Indian. The Government contended that the "allottee" did not become a full-fledged citizen of the United States under the particular statute involved, and therefore, still belonged to that class of Indians to which the sale of liquor was prohibited.

In the lower court the Judge had expressed the opinion that the United States still retained sufficient control over the Indian to curb his appetite for drink. The young attorney from Kansas, who appeared in a yellow tweed suit— no vest, flowing necktie, pink shirt and tan shoes—the most unique costume any lawyer ever wore during my time, paced

74

up and down before the Bench gesticulating and arguing somewhat to this effect:

"In Kansas we don't think there's anything to an Indian except his appetite for drink. But we don't care what the law is. We want to *know what he is.* If this man is an actual citizen and we refuse to sell him liquor, he sues us under the State's Equal Civil Rights Law. If he isn't a citizen, the Federal Government sues us for selling him the liquor. Now please tell us just what he is."

Mr. Justice Brewer, who was the recognized authority on all Indian matters, interrupted the young Kansas lawyer to ask:

"Mr. Counsellor, what do *you* think the status of an allottee is?"

The Kansas attorney stopped in front of Chief Justice Fuller and, spreading both his arms wide up in the air, exclaimed:

"If you fellows up there don't know, how do you think us fellows down here should know?"

The Court was stunned! Never before had it been described to its very face and in its own sacred precincts as— "You fellows up there."

The shocked expression on the face of dear Chief Justice Fuller will never be forgotten. Justice Holmes, shaking with laughter, buried his face in his arms on the Bench to hide his amusement, and there was a sort of dazed expression on the features of the other members of the Court. After a brief breathing spell, argument was resumed, and the Assistant Attorney General presented the Government's construction of the situation.

It was always a mystery to me why the Court decided the *Matter of Heff,** as the case was styled, in favor of the druggist. My only explanation is that it was largely owing to his lawyer's sheer audacity and his pink shirt. As time went on and other similar cases came up, this decision em-

* (197 U.S. 488.)

barrassed the Court. It was "distinguished" and its effect as *stare decisis* practically disappeared so far as the status of allottee Indians under other allotment statutes was concerned.

One day, however, this chicken came home to roost. In October, 1915 in response to the call of a case on the docket, which the respondent, relying on the success of the Kansas client of the pink-shirted attorney, had submitted on his brief, Assistant Attorney General Charles Warren asked the Court to allow him thirty minutes to argue the case on behalf of the Government which had brought the case up on appeal. He added, however, that he felt constrained to tell the Court he could not succeed in reversing the judgment of the Court below unless the Supreme Court would overrule itself.

Chief Justice White, who had been appointed by President Taft to "sit under the clock" after the death of Chief Justice Fuller, asked:

"What is the case you think should be over-ruled?"

"*Matter of Heff*," replied Mr. Warren.

After glancing inquiringly to his right and left, and apparently receiving affirmative responses, Chief Justice White said:

"Proceed."

And so on the last day of the term and in the last batch of decisions handed down during my Reportership that case was decided.* As it involved the status of an allottee Indian under exactly the same act as was involved therein, the Heff Case could not be distinguished as other cases arising under other statutes had been. Justice Van Devanter read the opinion, the concluding sentence of which was to the effect that the Court was constrained to hold the decision in the Heff Case not to be well founded and therefore it was overruled.

* (U.S. v. Nice 241 U.S. 591.)

Turning to the Marshal, who was sitting on my right, my comment was:

"Well, they got his tan shoes and his necktie long ago, and now they've got his pink shirt."

That was the end of the *Matter of Heff*.

Since then there have been numerous cases in which the Court, in my hearing, has overruled itself. A dramatic incident occurred one Monday in January, 1930 when the opinion in *Farmers Loan & Trust Co.* vs. *Minnesota* * was handed down. The case which was overruled appears in the second volume of my Reports under the title *Blackstone* vs. *Miller* † and related to the right of a State to tax intangible personal property belonging to a non-resident, but within its reach.

One Blackstone, whose name is perpetuated in the Chicago hotel of that name because it was built on the site of his residence, died a citizen of Illinois. As such all his personal estate, wheresoever situated, was included as taxable property in that State under the rule of *mobilia sequuntur personam*.

Included in the inventory of the estate was a large sum on deposit in a trust company in New York City. The State of New York claimed that this deposit was subject to an inheritance tax in New York. Disregarding therefore the *mobilia* rule under which it had been taxed in Illinois, a tax of more than $100,000 was levied for the benefit of the State of New York.

The suit was to avoid that tax. My friend, Edward W. Sheldon, Princeton '79, then counsel and afterwards president of the trust company in which the money was deposited, argued the case for the Blackstone Estate. Louis Marshall, one of the ablest lawyers of the New York Bar, appeared for Miller the Comptroller of New York State. The case was reached one afternoon in January, 1903 and

* (280 U.S. 204, 209.)
† (188 U.S. 189.)

Sheldon concluded his opening argument just as the Court adjourned.

While I was dining with Sheldon that evening he told me his opponent, Marshall, had complimented him on his opening, and, referring to questions asked by the Court, Marshall expressed the opinion that Sheldon would win the case. It still looked that way the next day when the case was finally submitted—but one never can tell.

Once, in reply to a question as to when and how the Supreme Court would decide a case my answer was:

"After nearly forty years' experience in listening to the arguments in the Supreme Court and the announcement of decisions on Monday mornings, the only response that can be given to that question is that you never can predict When, What or Why."

The decision in the *Blackstone* vs. *Miller* case confirmed this statement. Three weeks later in January, 1903, Justice Holmes announced the decision sustaining the tax. The decision explained that although it might be regrettable that one and the same State taxed on the inconsistency of *situs* as to non-residents and also of *mobilia sequuntur personam* as to residents, "these inconsistencies infringe no rule of *constitutional law;*" and that, while double taxation of the same subject matter was often inconvenient and sometimes unjust, it did not always and necessarily violate any provision of the Federal Constitution.

That decision stood as the law of the land under which millions in taxes were collected until 1930. Then came the remarkable incident of hearing one of the Justices read an opinion in which he denounced the reasoning of the then Senior Justice of the Court—who was sitting next to him—in a case decided twenty-six years before. The Justice who read this opinion ended with the statement that, as the views of the Court were exactly opposite to those previously expressed, the earlier case was "definitely overruled."

78

Mr. Justice Holmes dissented, but the law as established by the later case prevailed for the time being.

My friend Sheldon was immediately notified by wire that he had been vindicated on the stand he had taken twenty-six years before, as *Blackstone* vs. *Miller* had been definitely overruled that morning. In a nice letter Sheldon acknowledged my telegram. He requested me, however, to ask the Court how his client Mrs. Blackstone, could get back the $125,000 she had been obliged to pay the State of New York as the result of the original decision of the Court. Alas, that had gone forever.

During May 1939 another opinion was delivered by the Court in which the doctrine of *Blackstone* vs. *Miller* was to a great extent reinstated by a five to four decision.*

Long before my resignation my prediction had been that sooner or later, several cases decided during my term of office would be overruled. One of them was the Heff Case, in which the decision was, in my opinion, somewhat affected by the "pink shirt" element, and which was overruled just before my retirement. Another was this Blackstone Case which, in the opinion of myself as well as of others, was decided on an entirely erroneous basis.

While inconsistency may not always be illegal, when it results in an abnormal gain to the party practicing the inconsistencies, with a consequent abnormal loss to the other party—as was the case when New York State disregarded the *mobilia* rule as to non-residents and enforced it as to residents—it should then be outside the pale of municipal or constitutional law.

HEADNOTES

"WHO WRITES the headnotes in the cases in the United States Reports?" was a question often asked of me. Frequently my answer was:

"Nobody writes them. They just grow as *Topsy* did."

* (Curry v. McCanless 307 U.S. 357.)

As a matter of fact most of them were my own productions. Some were submitted to the Justices delivering the opinions, and some—most of them—were not. In a few cases the author of the opinion would send me the headnote. Every Justice had the opportunity, which was not seldom availed of, to make corrections in the advance sheets and the headnote would appear amended accordingly in the bound volume. Several of the Justices wanted the headnote submitted before the opinion appeared. Numerous letters in my files contain suggestions or corrections—some of them rather drastic—in regard to my first drafts sent to them for their approval or disapproval.

My publishers told me that Justice Gray always wrote the headnotes of his opinions himself and sent a copy to the Reporter and each of the publishers of the unofficial series. He evidently had no faith in the ability of anyone to digest and report his opinions properly. Some of the Justices, however, were averse even to pass on the headnotes because they wished to avoid all responsibility for them. One of them said to me:

"If the Court is not to be bound by the headnote, as declared in several opinions, no member of the Court should be in any way connected with its promulgation, as it is exclusively the expression of the ideas of the Reporter on what the opinion holds and the Court decides."

Justice Holmes once delivered an opinion in which he stated the above rule. He added that counsel citing a case had evidently read only the headnote, which, as Justice Holmes explained, conveyed an impression exactly opposite to that the opinion held. The title of this case had been so inaudibly uttered that it left me in suspense until relieved by obtaining the proof sheets from which the Justice had announced his opinion, which disclosed that the case cited had been decided long prior to my Reportership.

On another occasion, when it appeared as though Mr.

CHARLES HENRY BUTLER
1902

GEORGE SHIRAS, JR.

"JEFFERSON COLUMNS"

In the Capitol outside the Original Supreme Court Room
(later, the Library of the Supreme Court)

Justice White had been lulled into repose by the monotonous tone of argument, the counsel remarked—

"As held by Mr. Justice White"—in such and such a case, etc.

Without in any way changing his posture the Justice said:

"Mr. Justice White never held any such thing."

"But," returned the counsel, "let me read you the head-note which I have before me."

"If the headnote says any such thing as you stated," Mr. Justice White retorted, "the Reporter did not know his business."

Then, leaning forward, Mr. Justice White declared very forcibly that the opinion referred to held exactly contrary to what the counsel had said it held. Meanwhile my conscience was clear because that opinion also was delivered during my pre-Reportership days.

Just before the end of my Reportership several States enacted legislation to the effect that every opinion which was to go into the Reports should be accompanied by a syllabus, and that in subsequent decisions the Court should be bound by the syllabus and not by matter contained in the opinion. A judge in the mountainous section of one of the enacting States was heard to say:

"Writin' opinions is easy, but makin' up them syllibuses is hell."

If it was hell for the judge what must it have been for the Reporter?

There were no prescribed duties of my office requiring attendance in the Court Room. In fact most of my predecessors were seldom there. My attendance in Court, calculated on the number of personal appearances, probably exceeded the combined number of appearances of my three predecessors.

Chief Justice White told me once that some Justices thought the Reporter should be present at all sessions of the Court. While disclaiming their opinion as his own, he sought to know my reaction. He was quite surprised to learn that while my percentage of attendance was not quite up to Ivory Soap's 99.44 per cent pure, it was well over 90 per cent. Nor did it take me long to show the Chief Justice that it was impossible for the Reporter to do any work in the Court Room; that the headnotes could not be prepared until after the cases had been decided, and the opinions delivered; and that the Government paid for an office for the Reporter in which to prepare and edit the Reports. This question was never referred to again, nor were any rules regarding the Reporter's attendance in the Court promulgated during my term of office.

Occasionally it was necessary to call the attention of the justices to typographical errors in the opinions as handed down by them. The following is reminiscent of one such instance:—

Washington, D. C., June 19, 1913.

Charles Henry Butler, Esq.,

   ·Reporter, United States Supreme Court,

      Washington, D. C.

My dear Mr. Butler:-

   Yes, it is obvious that the word defendants in the last line of the first page of No. 320 should be plaintiffs.

                  Yours very truly,

                  E. D. White

At another time an interesting incident with Chief Justice White occurred regarding the inclusion in the Reports of summaries of arguments by counsel. To appreciate the situation, one should know that although the contracts between the publishers and my predecessor, as well as the original contract with me, had been on a per volume basis, that arrangement had long since been changed by my insistence

82

SUPREME COURT OF THE UNITED STATES

upon a lump sum per annum, whatever the number of volumes might be. These arrangements were between the publishers and the Reporters, and members of the Court knew nothing about them, except as they might come to their attention incidentally.

On this occasion the Chief Justice, seemingly somewhat perturbed, informed me that some members of the Court felt the Reporter was unduly "padding" the Reports by the insertion of the argument of counsel, presumably to insure the issuance of four volumes instead of three in each term, thus increasing his profits from the publication of the Reports. He was surprised at my immediate request that he announce on the following Monday an Order of the Court directing the Reporter to discontinue the inclusion of any matter except the opinions, the headnote of the case and the names of counsel.

Such an order, it was explained, would enable the Reporter to keep the Reports down to three volumes per term, which would be to his advantage in saving him from $500 to $1,000 per annum by so reducing his expenses. As far as the Reporter was concerned, the publication of four instead of three volumes per term was a loss rather than a profit, because of the added expense to him of preparation of the summaries of arguments, and of the proofreading and indexing of four rather than three volumes.

The attention of the Chief Justice was called also to the fact that the space filled by argument of counsel was far less in my Reports than in those of my predecessors. In the Bell Telephone Case 584 pages were used for argument of counsel. In the famous suit of *Gibbons* vs. *Wheaton* in the ninth of Wheaton, the case begins on page 1 and the pages from there up to 186 are devoted to "abstracts" of the arguments of the distinguished counsel who appeared for the various parties.

This colloquy with the Chief Justice ended by his saying: "My dear Butler, you do not know how you have relieved me, and how much pleasure it will give to tell the Brethren tomorrow that it is worth more to the Reporter to publish three volumes instead of four."

On the walls of my cubby hole of an office, just off the Court Room, hung portraits of all my predecessors except Judge Davis, who had presented the paintings to the Court. They were copies of originals hanging elsewhere. Judge Davis had small photographs made of them and enclosed them all within one frame; the composite was presented to Chief Justice Fuller. After Chief Justice Fuller's death, his very charming daughter, Mrs. Hugh Wallace, now also deceased, gave it to me, and it is reproduced as one of the illustrations in this book. The space for the portrait of Judge Davis was occupied by a photograph of him. His portrait, originally designed to complete the group, was not presented to the Court until after his death in 1907.

All these portraits were removed to the new Supreme Court Building, and hang in the Reporter's Office, where there is also a rather small photograph of myself.

Chapter VIII

RULES AND CUSTOMS OF THE SUPREME COURT

RULES AND CUSTOMS of the Supreme Court have been greatly modified since my appointment as the Reporter of its Decisions in 1902.

For many years Mr. Justice Gray was the sartorial dictator of the Court. According to my friend, Marshal Wright, he insisted on strict formal dress for everyone connected with the Court, or appearing before it. Major Wright told me that in order to help out unfortunate counsel, who had come unprepared to meet the strict dress requirements insisted upon by Mr. Justice Gray, he had acquired, somehow or other, several old frock coats of various sizes, and kept them in a closet in his office so they might be donned by counsel otherwise unprepared.

Until the Court moved into its new building, the Marshal of the Court always conducted them from the Robing Room across the north to the south corridor of the Capitol into the Court Room. The Marshal was always attired in his frock coat for this ceremony. One Monday morning, however, the cleaner disappointed him and did not return his frock coat until after twelve o'clock. This obliged the Marshal to lead the procession wearing a short, but fortunately, dark coat.

The Marshal told me that Mr. Justice Gray summoned him, and notwithstanding the Marshal's explanation, demanded an apology, with an intimation that if it ever happened again, the Court would ask for his resignation. Happily it never did happen again. Even if such a thing had happened again before the death of Mr. Justice Gray it is doubtful whether the dire punishment threatened would have been inflicted on anyone who was so much loved and respected by all connected with the Court as was Marshal John Montgomery Wright.

My court attire was the regulation Prince Albert coat until the last few years of my term when it was changed to a black cutaway. My last frock coat, as had its predecessors when they were discarded, became the property of a colored clergyman, who not so long ago informed me that he was still wearing it every Sunday morning when he delivered his sermon.

For some time after the decease of Justice Gray, counsel continued to appear either in frock coats or cutaways. The Attorney General's office still adheres to the latter dress. Other counsel generally wear dark clothes, though very often of much shorter length than the old-time frock coat or the present cutaway.

In late years, however, counsel have appeared in much lighter garb than ever was known in the olden days. In one case, as related in a previous chapter, counsel appeared in an olive-yellow tweed suit, tan shoes, pink shirt and no vest. He was permitted to address the Court, however, because he came from Kansas and had an important message to deliver. In another case, by the direction of Chief Justice Taft, the Clerk, during the luncheon hour, requested an Assistant State Attorney General, either to put on a vest or else button up his coat so as not to expose quite so much of his shirt to view.

In respect to time allowed for argument, there has also been a great modification of the rules. Based on their own remarks, made in my hearing, Chief Justice Fuller and Justices Harlan and Brewer considered that counsel should have ample time to present the cases of their clients and constantly opposed any effort to limit them.

Mr. Justice Holmes was all for cutting the time down, and

more than once told me that he was never influenced by oral arguments, but considered the cases wholly on the briefs. In nearly every case counsel were allowed two hours a side, which, if availed of, would take a full day for each case. Frequently extra time was given. In some of the anti-trust cases, such as those involving the United States Steel Company, the Standard Oil Company, and the International Harvester Company, each case was allowed six hours. Thus a single case occupied three entire days.

The two-hours a side Court rule applied to cases that came up on writ of error or appeal based on a Federal question being involved. To these cases the full time was permitted, even if the writs or the appeals were founded on very doubtful grounds. So long as the cases could not be affirmed or dismissed on motion for lack of Federal question, no matter how ephemeral the basis might be, full time had to be granted if counsel so desired, as counsel generally did.

When Mr. Justice White became Chief Justice, he instituted a new rule under which, if an appeal could not be dismissed, or the writ denied as frivolous, it was placed on the "Summary Docket." Only thirty minutes a side was allowed for cases on this docket. After a few cases placed on it had been dismissed with ten per cent damages, writs of errors and appeals of that nature were greatly discouraged. All this was done away with by the rules Chief Justice Taft promulgated after the Act of 1925, under which nearly all those cases come up by writs of certiorari.

The Court saved time often by announcing, after the petitioner or appellant had made his opening argument, which failed to support his contention, that it would not hear the respondent. This was equivalent to saying that the moving party had so completely failed to sustain his case that it would be a waste of time to hear arguments by counsel representing the other side. This was a great relief to the respondent, although it was often a disappointment not to be able to address the Supreme Court of the United States.

Mr. William B. Hornblower, of New York, told me that on his second wedding tour he arranged that a case in which he represented the respondent be argued before the Supreme Court while he was in Washington. This was, he said, for the double purpose of having his new bride hear him argue a case before the Supreme Court; and incidentally to be able to charge with propriety at least part of his expenses as disbursements. Thus he followed the example of *Mrs. John Gilpin*, who, although on pleasure bent, still had a frugal mind.

The plaintiff in error, having demonstrated in the opening argument the lack of merit in his case, the Chief Justice said:

"The Court does not care to hear the respondent."

My friend Hornblower had just stood up to address the Court; and so far as he was concerned this statement by the Chief Justice was a relief. He informed me, however, that Mrs. Hornblower, who was all agog to hear him make his argument, never forgave the Court.

On another occasion Matthew Carpenter, a well known practitioner of the law, presented his case with similar ineffectiveness, and the Court made an announcement like the one just quoted. The opposing attorney, who was very deaf, could not hear what the Chief Justice said. So he whispered to Carpenter as he sat down:

"Matt, what did the Chief Justice say?"

Matt, who naturally was not at all pleased with the Court's action, replied in a voice resounding through the Court Room:

"He said he would rather give you the damn case than hear you talk."

A traditional story of Marshal Wright's was that when Jeremiah—otherwise 'Jerry'—Wilson began an elaborate opening by citing many of the fundamental authorities, he was interrupted by an Associate Justice who said that

88

Mr. Wilson ought to take it for granted that the Court knew some elementary law. To this 'Jerry' Wilson replied:

"Your Honors, that was the mistake I made in the Court below."

Another of Marshal Wright's stories told how counsel spread out a large map. One of the Justices asked what it was, and counsel answered that it was a bird's-eye view of the scene where the cause of action arose. Another Justice interposed:

"Well, as we are not birds, you can take it away."

Mr. Justice Shiras, who at times was inclined to be a wag, was credited with saying to counsel, during the argument of the Benedict Collar Button Case in which a hump in the middle of the shank was relied on to justify the patent, that if a certain question were answered affirmatively, he might be in favor of sustaining the patent. When counsel asked what the question was, the Justice answered:

"Will this hump prevent the collar button from rolling under the bureau when you drop it?"

It took some time to get the Court back to listen seriously to the argument.

A still older story sometimes told about the Court and pinned on some particular attorney, on some particular occasion, before some particular Justice, is that when counsel stated a conclusion of law, one of the Justices said:

"That is not the law."

"It was until your Honor spoke," counsel replied.

It is my belief that record of a similar conversation can be found in a little volume on one of the shelves of the New York Bar Association library, entitled, "Annals of Westminster Hall," which was published about 150 years ago. Nevertheless it's a good story whoever the judge and counsel may have been and whenever and wherever it originated.

In a book published about the Justices of the Supreme Court there is a story of long ago. In a little cabinet in the Robing Room was kept some material by which the Justices might be refreshed after an arduous session on the Bench. It seems, however, that a rule had been made that the contents of the cabinet should be opened only in case it was raining.

On one occasion, the story continues, upon retiring from the Bench, a certain Justice remarked that as it had been a hard day it might be well to resort to the cabinet.

"But it is not raining," said another Justice.

Thereupon Chief Justice Marshall looked out the window and then observed:

"No, it is not raining here, but it is probably raining somewhere in the jurisdiction."

This justified opening the cabinet.

That is a good and oft-told story; but there is an addition thereto possibly not so widely known to others as to myself. One evening when several Justices were present at a gathering at 1535 Eye Street, in answer to my inquiry as to the authenticity of the story Mr. Justice Brewer said:

"Why, Mr. Reporter, the story is not only true, but you ought to know that the Court sustained the constitutionality of the acquisition of the Philippines so as to be sure of having plenty of rainy seasons."

Whether or not the historic cabinet of the Robing Room in the Capitol was transported to the new building now occupied by the august tribunal has never been disclosed to my knowledge.

The temperature of the Court Room in the Capitol was very difficult to regulate. This difficulty was increased by the various views of the different Justices as to what its proper temperature should be. The regulation of the heat had always been under the control of the Marshal.

There is a traditional story anent this particular matter, which is generally ascribed to Justices Gray and Bradley. Justice Gray, who weighed more than 250 pounds, it is said, always wanted the thermometer kept below 70 degrees, while Justice Bradley, who was a very thin man, and of much lower weight, always wanted it kept up to nearly 80 degrees.

One day as Justice Bradley was going behind the screen back of the Bench, with his gown wrapped round him and apparently shivering with the cold, he pointed to an open window and said to the Marshal:

"What d——d fool opened that window?"

"That window," answered Major Wright, "was opened, Your Honor, by the order of Mr. Justice Gray."

"I thought so—I thought so. Shut it up and keep it shut," snapped the irate Justice Bradley and went to his seat on the Bench.

CHAPTER IX

DECISIONS OF THE SUPREME COURT

THE INSULAR CASES were argued and decided before my Reportership. They were the cases of which *Mr. Dooley* said:

"Mr. Justice Brown delivered the opinion of the Court and only eight Justices dissented."

As a matter of fact in the Porto Rico Case,* which involved the status of that Territory under Article X of the Treaty of Peace, Mr. Justice Brown delivered "the conclusion and *judgment* of the Court," and there was no *opinion* of the Court.

Although a majority of the Court agreed that Porto Rico was not foreign territory, a majority did not agree as to what was its exact status. The predominant question in that case was whether the acquired territory had become so fully incorporated into the United States that constitutional rights similar to those enjoyed by residents in other territories were possessed by inhabitants of Porto Rico. Justice White wrote the longest opinion and three other Justices concurred with him.

In the early part of the 1904 term, an appeal came to the Court in a criminal case, in which a man had been convicted of conducting a disorderly house in a city of Alaska, and had been fined $500. His appeal was based on the plea of the unconstitutionality of a law of the Territory of Alaska permitting a majority verdict of a jury instead of requiring a

* (Downes v. Bidwell 182 U.S. 244, 247.)

unanimous verdict. This was known as the Rassmussen Case.*

The principal issue was, therefore, whether Alaska had become so incorporated into the United States that its inhabitants were entitled to all the constitutional rights as citizens of those Territories which had been incorporated. The records and briefs on both sides did not exceed one hundred pages.

In the Insular Cases there were more than one thousand pages; for in these cases numerous and distinguished counsel appeared. The Rassmussen Case was submitted without argument. Since the Insular Cases the personnel of the Court had undergone some changes. Justice Holmes had replaced Justice Gray, and Justice Shiras had been replaced by Justice Day. In one way or other, millions of dollars as well as civil rights were involved in the Insular Cases; the Rassmussen Case involved simply the legality of a $500 fine. Both cases, however, concerned the constitutional rights of people either of, or under control of, the United States. The little $500 case received as much attention in the Conference Room of the Court as did the Insular Cases.

When at last the decision was announced, the Court held that Alaska had been incorporated into the territory of the United States. In so doing the Court adopted Justice White's views as to what constituted such incorporation, as stated by him in the Downes Case three years before, when he held that the Philippines had not been incorporated. Three separate opinions were delivered, but this time Justice White had a majority of the Court with him.

Immediately after he had declared his opinion, one of the pages told me that Justice White wanted to see me behind the Bench. My approach back of the screen was from one side and Justice White's from the other. As he came towards me, the breeze from the open window blowing out his gown, he was flourishing the proof sheets of his opinion

* (197 U.S. 516.)

in one hand and shaking the fist of the other at me, it seemed. Then he exclaimed in a voice that was probably heard by all who were on the other side of the screen:

"Butler, now *Downes* vs. *Bidwell* is the opinion of the Court and I want you to make it so appear in your report of this case."

To Justice White it was as great a victory as winning his first case in the Supreme Court would be for a youthful attorney; and he was bound that everybody should know that his views as to incorporation or non-incorporation of acquired territory in the United States had become the law of the land.

As I have said, Mr. Justice Holmes told me he had hardly ever been influenced by the oral orgument, but relied on the record in the case, to some extent assisted by the briefs. On one occasion, however, he was so influenced by the oral delivery of a dissent in a case in which he was on the majority side until he heard the dissent orally presented, that, from his seat on the Bench he directed the Clerk to add his name to those concurring in the dissent, thus making the decision five to four. Had it been originally five to four, instead of six to three, his action would have changed the judgment of the Court, and it would be hard to tell what would have happened in such an event. This is the only recorded case in my experience in which a Justice of the Supreme Court changed his final stand in the Conference Room after the opinion of the Court had been announced from the Bench.

The method of announcement of the decisions of the Court sometimes led to misunderstandings as to what had been actually decided. A notable instance was that of the Chicago Traction Franchise Cases. The principal question was whether an act passed by the Illinois Legislature had extended the charter and franchise of the corporation. The

94

Court's opinion was awaited with intense interest as the value of the widely held stock of the Traction Company depended on it.*

Justice Day delivered the opinion of the Court. In order that there might be no misunderstanding of the conclusions reached by the Court, he wrote out the brief announcement which he intended to make, as the opinion was too long to be read. Copies of his written statement were given to the Clerk to be handed to the news-reporters awaiting the decision. Under telegraph company rules, what are called "flashes," that is a very few words in regard to an important public matter, may be rushed over the wires ahead of already filed messages. Mr. Justice Day's statement was delivered to the news-reporters the moment he began to read it. But the significance of his first two lines was entirely misapprehended.

Whether the corporation's charter was extended was one thing; whether its franchise was extended was another. The State had denied that either the charter or the franchise had been extended beyond a date which had long since expired. The remarks of Justice Day began with "the Act of 1859, extending the charter of the Chicago Traction Company—"

As the Justice read these words, the reporters, who were holding copies of the statement in their hands, yet had not read them, waited to hear no further from Justice Day and rushed their "flashes": "Traction wins."

Justice Day's statement, however, added: "but that Act did not extend the franchise."

Traction had lost, not won.

It took a long time to straighten out the error. Meanwhile Traction stock kept soaring on the Exchange until the "flashes" could be contradicted and the real state of affairs understood. After adjournment, Justice Day handed me a copy of his statement, saying that he thought it was plain enough. He might better have started the statement

* (Blair v. City of Chicago 201 U.S. 400.)

with—"The Act of 1859 did *not* extend the franchise, although it did extend the charter of the Traction Company." Then the "flash" would have read—"Traction loses"; but it was too late to make the correction.

To recall a similar instance: Justice McKenna was reading his opinion in a suit brought by the Western Union Telegraph Company against the Pennsylvania Railroad Company for damages sustained in the cutting down of its poles and wires after having made an exclusive contract with the Postal Telegraph Company. The newspaper-reporters guessed, while listening to the reading of the opinion, that the Western Union Telegraph Company had won the suit; that was my feeling, too, until almost at the conclusion of the opinion, when, to the surprise of many of us, judgment was rendered for the Pennsylvania Railroad Company.*

As the opinion was a lengthy one, some of the news-reporters had sent out dispatches to the effect that the Western Union was the victor. The consequence was, the stock exchanges being open, that prices of the stocks of both companies were affected by the erroneous guesses of over-zealous newspapermen.

The danger of not understanding the full purport and effect of the decisions is now obviated. The Clerk of the Court has at hand a number of copies of the proof sheets from which the decisions are announced. A page distributes these proof sheets to the reporters who can scan the final paragraphs and correctly transmit their contents. A pneumatic tube, through which the opinions are sent, connects the desk of each news-reporter in the Court Room with the desk of his collaborator in the press room on the floor below. The auditors in the Court Room, however, have to await the completion of the announcement before being sure of what is the final judgment of the Court.

That the value of stocks on the exchanges can be seriously

* (Western Union v. Pennsylvania R.R. Co. 195 U.S. 540.)

THE SUPREME COURT OF THE UNITED STATES
1903

Standing, left to right: Justice Oliver Wendell Holmes, Justice Rufus W. Peckham, Justice Joseph McKenna, and Justice William R. Day.

Seated, left to right: Justice Henry B. Brown, Justice John Marshall Harlan, Chief Justice Melville W. Fuller, Justice David J. Brewer, Justice Edward D. White.

THE REPORTERS OF THE SUPREME COURT
PRIOR TO CHARLES HENRY BUTLER

affected by decisions of the Supreme Court was demonstrated in the New York City 80 cent Gas Case, which had been declared unconstitutional in the lower court. The appeal was argued in the Supreme Court in November, 1908. A suit which involved very similar issues regarding the rates established in Knoxville, Tennessee, was argued about the same time.

For seven Mondays after the New York case had been argued, a New York lawyer friend of mine sat within the Bar, listening attentively to the decisions. Early in January 1909 Justice Moody read an opinion adverse to the Knoxville Case.* My friend immediately disappeared, but returned shortly to hear Justice Peckham announce the decision refusing to set aside the New York ordinance.†

When the Court opened Consolidated Gas was selling at about 160, and my friend, as he told me afterward, had left sufficient margin with his brokers either to buy 1000 shares of Consolidated Gas, or to "go short" of the market for the same number of shares with a stop order to sell or cover at ten points' profit.

Before the New York Stock Exchange closed that day, Consolidated Gas had dropped to 130 and my friend, who had given his order to sell the stock short had covered it by buying it in, and had made $10,000 on the day's transaction. This, he said, had made it very worth while for him to come from New York to Washington every one of the seven Mondays on which the Court had sat and delivered opinions between the time of the argument and the decision of the case.

Some of the most interesting cases that have come before the Supreme Court were those between the States themselves. Since the Eleventh Amendment to the Constitution was adopted even the Supreme Court cannot enter-

---

* (Knoxville v. Water Co. 212 U.S. 1.)
† (Willcox v. Consolidated Gas Co. 212 U.S. 19.)

tain a suit by an individual, or a private corporation, against a State. Nor can individuals bring suits against the States in their own courts, except when consent has been specially given. When a State defaults on payment of principal or interest on its bonds, it is therefore very difficult to enforce collection in the courts. Many efforts have been made; most of them, however, have proved futile.

There was a notable exception during the period of my Reportership. A prominent banking firm in New York City had a large block of bonds issued by the State of North Carolina. These bonds differed from the ordinary issue of State bonds in that the entire issue was secured by the entire Capital Stock of the North Carolina Railroad Company. Each $1,000 bond bore the endorsement that it was secured by ten shares of stock of the North Carolina Railroad Company.

No interest was paid on the bonds for many years, nor was the principal paid when it became due. The Constitution gives the Supreme Court jurisdiction over suits between States and various efforts were made to avail of this jurisdiction; but as no State owned any of the bonds, no suit could be entertained by the Court.

In order to get up a case within the jurisdiction of the Court, the owner of a block of bonds presented ten of them, together with the unpaid coupons thereon, to the State of South Dakota.* This State brought suit against North Carolina for the full amount due. It is not my intention to recount all the details of that suit. The jurisdiction of the Court was challenged on the ground that the constitutional jurisdiction did not include suits on bonds issued on the faith of the State's honor to recognize the obligation. The petition of South Dakota to bring the case into the Court was well argued with the result that the Court—by a narrow margin—accepted jurisdiction to the extent of determining the disposition and application of the collateral securing the

* (South Dakota v. North Carolina 192 U.S. 286, 322.)

bonds. It reserved the question of jurisdiction as to any deficiency there might be in case the collateral did not cover the debt.

It became evident on the argument of the main issue that the object of the donation by the owner of this block of bonds was not actuated by his philanthropy and desire to advance the interests of South Dakota. His real objective was to obtain an adjudication that the entire $1,000,000 of stock should be sold to satisfy the amount due on the whole issue, the proceeds to be applied *pro rata*, not only to the bonds in suit, but also to the balance of the issue.

Whatever the object of the suit may have been, it was defeated. The Court held, in an opinion written by Mr. Justice Brewer, that the State did owe the debt, and that the creditor had a right to have the collateral sold to satisfy the obligation. But the Court also held that each bond was a separate obligation and that ten shares of stock were allocable as collateral for each bond.

The decree therefore provided that the Marshal of the Supreme Court of the United States should sell on the east steps of the Capitol in Washington 100 shares of the stock of the North Carolina Railroad, the proceeds of the sale to be applied towards the total amount of the debt due to the State of South Dakota, and report to be made to the Supreme Court what, if any, balance remained due on the obligation. The Court reserved determination of what further proceedings would be taken, or whether judgment would be entered, in case the yield of the sale of the stock was less than the amount due.

The day before the sale was to take place the State of North Carolina paid the amount of the judgment in full; and this ended the case so far as the Supreme Court of the United States was concerned.

GOLD CLAUSE CASE DECISIONS

In 1935, after the Gold Clause Cases * had been argued and submitted, there was much and constant speculation not only as to how things would be decided, but also when. Each Saturday, after the Court had concluded its usual conference, announcements in the newspapers and by radio commentators were made as to the prospects that the decisions would be made public the following Monday. Every Monday the Court Room and the adjacent corridors in the Capitol—where the Court still held its sessions—were crowded with visitors eager to hear the news. On two occasions after the close of the Saturday conference, the Chief Justice authorized a statement that the decisions in the Gold Cases would not be announced on the following Monday. When he did not authorize such a statement one Saturday after the conference, it was logical, and as it transpired, proper, to expect that the decisions would be given out on the following Monday.

On that eventful morning my office had a telephone inquiry as to whether the decisions surely would be announced that day. The telephone inquirer said that it was very important for him to have a definite answer, which of course it was impossible to give. However, we devised a plan to relieve the anxiety of our friend, who desired to cable his London correspondent before twelve o'clock.

At half past eleven one of our staff connected a pay station in the Capitol with our inquirer, another stood at the door of the Court Room where he could watch me, so that on my giving him a designated signal he could tell his colleague in the telephone booth to give our New York friend the prearranged message:

"The ladies have arrived."

My constant attendance on Monday mornings during fourteen years had taught me that if the seats reserved for

* (294 U.S. 240.)

100

the families or the friends of the Justices were occupied by members of the family before the Court opened, something out of the ordinary was likely to happen. Our friend in New York had been informed that if several of the ladies of the Court should occupy those reserved seats, it could safely be predicted that something out of the ordinary was going to happen.

While correctly assuming that no Justice of the Supreme Court of the United States ever discloses to his wife what any decision of the Court may be, or when it will be announced, certainly no reason exists why he should not intimate to her on a Monday morning that if she should by any chance attend the session of the Court that morning, she might hear something interesting.

The pre-arranged message "The ladies have arrived," transmitted to our inquirer in New York, proved to be just as illuminating as though it had been to the effect that the decisions in the Gold Cases would be announced that morning. It was an eventful day in the Court and one long to be remembered.

SUPREME COURT INCIDENT

DURING MY fourteen years' experience as Reporter of the Court and my frequent appearances in the Court Room, on only one occasion was there any exhibition of an intoxicated member of the Bar endeavoring to impress the Court with his eloquence. It happened, however, that on this occasion Ambassador Bryce had accompanied me for his first visit to the Court and occupied a seat within the Bar next to my desk.

An able member of the New York Bar, but who was inclined at times to dine "not wisely, but too well," was present that morning for the very unusual purpose of asking the Court to explain its decision made the week before on a motion in a pending case in which he was counsel.

101

March 13, 1935

2101 CONNECTICUT AVENUE
WASHINGTON

Dear Mr. Butler,

I think you make sufficient proof of your good will toward the Court when you visit us Monday mornings and listen with such patience to the reading of opinions.

Today, however, you submitted cumulative proof when you left a fine

---

Since the termination of my Reportership it has been my custom to attend the Monday sessions of the Court when decisions are handed down, and occasionally to supply the Justices

102

apple for each of us, from
the Chief Justice at the top
to the junior associate at
the bottom —

If I had to choose
between the opinions and
the apples, I know where
my choice would fall —

Many thanks and cordial
greetings   Faithfully yours

            Benjamin N Cardozo

Charles Harry Butler, Esq.

---

with apples grown in my Montsweag Farm Orchards, in Maine.
Mr. Justice Cardozo's letter, here reproduced, comments on the
relative merits of apples and decisions—from his point of view.

Before the opening of the session, the Marshal, who knew that the gentleman had been a long-time acquaintance of mine, and realizing that the effects of the dissipation of the previous evening had not been entirely effaced by a night's slumber, asked me to unite with him in suggesting a postponement of his motion until the next morning.

To this our New York friend agreed and left the Marshal's office to return to his hotel room, as we supposed. It was rather disconcerting to us, therefore, to see him re-enter the Court Room and, on motions being called for, to approach the desk in front of Chief Justice Fuller—to whom a warning had been given by the Marshal as to the gentleman's condition—and solemnly state that he rose to ask the Court to explain what it meant by its decision announced a week before in regard to his motion.

At this point Ambassador Bryce inquired of me whether the gentleman was a friend of mine, which resulted in the admission of a slight acquaintance. The Chief Justice meanwhile had asked counsel what he meant by his motion, to which came the reply that the decision was wholly unintelligible, and counsel could not proceed in the case unless the meaning was explained. The Chief Justice quietly responded:

"This Court does not explain its decisions. Counsel must interpret them for themselves."

"Then," returned the counsel in a highly rhetorical tone, "this Court must take the responsibility for making such a decision."

To this Chief Justice Fuller replied:[1]

"This Court for more than a century has been accustomed to take the responsibility for its decisions."

Thus ended one of the most remarkable colloquies between counsel and the Court heard during my attendance.

My friend made his exit from the Court Room and as he passed my desk said:

"Charles Henry, you see I'm all right."

Thereupon the Ambassador observed to me:

"You seem to know the gentleman pretty well."

This, however, was not the *finale* of the episode. A few moments later Ambassador Bryce and I, having gone from the Court Room by the side exit where we were joined by Mrs. Bryce and one of my sisters, left the elevator on the ground floor. Simultaneously my bibulous friend, starting at the top of the stairway directly opposite the elevator, tumbled all the way down and landed right at the feet of the Ambassador. Mr. Bryce availed himself of the situation to remark again on my probable close acquaintance with the gentleman from New York.

It is only fair to say that the case of which this episode was merely an interlude, was a very important one, involving intricate questions of Admiralty and Maritime Law. Further it must be stated that a few weeks afterward, the case was argued on its merits by my friend and his associates in a masterful manner—especially as to his own argument— and was decided in their favor.

He had appeared before the Court many times in connection with Admiralty cases and was remarkably successful. While some of his friends knew of his elbow-lifting proclivity, the incident above related was the only evidence of it in the Supreme Court.

There was, however, a story to the effect that once when he opened a case in one of the lower courts in a rather confused manner, the opposing counsel made request of the Court that his learned friend should present his case a little more fully, whereupon the presiding judge said:

"While your opponent may not have fully *detailed* his case, it must be conceded that he has made a *full* presentation."

CHAPTER X

THE WRIT OF CERTIORARI

WHEN ST. PAUL told the Corinthians that the wonderful Gospel he preached was "to the Jews a stumbling block and to the Greeks foolishness," he was not expressing any doubt in regard to the truth and efficacy of the Gospel. He was referring to the difficulty of making his Grecian and Hebraic listeners understand it. This attempt on my part to explain *certiorari* might be described by paraphrasing the great missionary's remark in regard to his far more interesting subject:

"*Certiorari* is to the laymen foolishness and to the lawyers a stumbling block."

There is no reason why laymen would understand what *certiorari* means or anything about that process for invoking this extraordinary jurisdiction of the Supreme Court of the United States. Few of them know, or need to know anything about it. Of the 150,000 persons admitted to practise law at the Bar of their respective States, probably less than twenty per cent are members of the Bar of the Supreme Court of the United States.

Of this percentage only a fraction ever attends any session of the Court except when admitted to its Bar. A still smaller percentage ever has a single case on its docket. Hence comparatively few lawyers have any real and comprehensive practical knowledge of the fundamental rules relating to the writ of *certiorari,* and the practice of the Court with regard to it.

If, however, occasion should arise when one needs help, the Clerk of the Court and his staff will always, with efficiency and courtesy, afford all possible assistance to guide the steps of the seeker in the right direction so as to avoid pitfalls along the way.

That the Chief Justice of the United States knows more about the writ of *certiorari* and its use in connection with the Supreme Court of the United States than the President of the United States may know, was demonstrated in the verbal battle between the two in 1937. President Franklin D. Roosevelt declared in one of his messages that many suitors in the Supreme Court did not have a real opportunity to be heard. He justified this remark by stating that about 80 per cent of the petitions for writs of *certiorari* to review decisions of lower courts were denied, thus preventing defeated litigants from presenting their respective appeals to the highest court of the land.

Shortly after this presidential enunciation Chief Justice Hughes, at the meeting of the American Law Institute in May, 1937, gave an accurate and lucid explanation of the action of the Court in regard to *certiorari*. He said:

"We have thus far during the current term granted 123 petitions for *certiorari* and denied 583. The number granted is close to the usual percentage of petitions which have been found entitled to a grant under our rules. These rules are designed to carry out the intent of the Jurisdictional Act of 1925 in insuring the hearing of cases that are important in the interest of the law. That is, where review by the Court of last resort is needed to secure harmony of decision in the lower Courts of Appeal, and the appropriate settlement of questions of general importance so that the system of Federal Justice may be appropriately administered.

"We are liberal in the application of our rules and *certiorari* is always granted if four Justices think it should be, and, not infrequently, when three or even two Justices strongly urge the grant."

Let me add to this succinct statement of Chief Justice Hughes that in nearly every case enough extra copies of the record in the Courts below are printed so that the defeated party has on hand the necessary copies for the record that must accompany the petition. This greatly reduces the expense of preparing the record for the application. The defeated party, naturally, files the petition asking the high Court to review the decision, hoping, as Chief Justice Hughes has said, that at least a substantial minority of the Court may think it proper to grant the petition, and at the same time well aware that the great majority of petitions are denied.

This method of review by *certiorari,* instead of by right of appeal or writ of error, was originally instituted by the Judiciary Act of 1891 for Patents only. Now, however, it is controlled by the later Act of 1925. Under the Act of 1925 the Court also exercises its right to review, not only judgments of Federal Courts, but also of State Courts when Federal questions are involved, in addition to the right of appeal from State Courts in certain federal questions.

The Court is under no statutory obligation to grant the petition. It has more than once declared that issuance of the writ is a right given to the Court to enable it to review the decisions of the lower Courts in order to determine issues of national importance, and to decide which one of the differing decisions of the lower Courts should be approved for the future administration of the law.

Many thousand petitions for writs of *certiorari* have been filed, submitted to and acted upon by the Court; but in very few instances have any opinions been written either as to the granting or denial of the petitions. Marshal Wright told an interesting story about Chief Justice Fuller writing a single opinion, showing why the writ should be granted, as the case evidently fell within the classes intended by Congress to be reviewed by *certiorari.*

According to the Marshal's story it leaked out that there was much discussion in the Conference Room about the propriety of writing any such opinion. The Chief Justice, however, adhered to his idea and wrote and announced his opinion. Justice Gray, who was the leader of the opposition, is reported to have said then:

"Very well, now write an opinion in which—although we all think that possibly the judgment rendered by the Court below may have been wrong—we do not think it is of sufficient importance to be entitled to review by this Court."

This evidently settled the matter as there does not seem to have been any other opinion ever written for the grant or denial of a petition for a writ of *certiorari*.

One reason for this "no opinion" policy is that, as the Court has frequently declared, its action on the petition is not to be regarded as an indication of its attitude on the merits of the case. The granting of the petition can be regarded only as a hopeful sign of a possible reversal of the judgment below when the case is finally submitted to the high Court on its merits.

The Court has often announced that denial of a petition is not to be construed as an affirmance of the judgment below even though generally it has practically that effect; nor does it create a precedent under the doctrine of *stare decisis*. Even when the citation is followed by a parenthetical addition—"*certiorari* denied"—it is not justifiable to call it an expression of opinion by the Supreme Court. Nor does this denial of the petition in any one case preclude the Court from subsequently granting—as has happened on more than one occasion—the petition in a case in which the issues are similar, or even identical.

It can be seen therefore how embarrassing it would be for the Court to place on record the reasons for granting or for denying a petition. Perhaps it shows also the applicability of the paraphrased remark of St. Paul, and the difficulties encountered in my humble efforts to explain to my readers the practice of the Supreme Court of the United States in the exercise of this extraordinary power. The exercise of this power undoubtedly has greatly aided in the reconciliation of the conflicting views of the numerous Federal and State Courts by which law and justice are administered throughout the country.

As to the "no opinion" rule of the Court, Chief Justice

1301 CLIFTON STREET
WASHINGTON, D. C.

February 10th, 1917.

Mr. Charles Henry Butler,
1537 Eye Street,
Washington, D. C.

My dear Mr. Butler:

I have your favor of the 8th instant, calling attention to the rules of the Supreme Court concerning the consideration of petitions for writs of certiorari.

It will give me great pleasure to call the matter to the attention of the court at its early convenience.

Very truly yours,

William R. Day

Letter from Mr. Justice Day

Fuller became an ardent disciple of Justice Gray. During my Reportership in three cases similarly entitled *Standard Oil Company* vs. *the United States* (though each case involved a different issue) petitions for *certiorari* were denied. All petitions were reported on the same page of the same issue of advance sheets of the then current volume of the Reports. For identification as to the subject matter therein involved a note was made as to each case. Chief Justice Fuller immediately called my attention to the fact, and saying that there should not be even a note of this nature, instructed me to eliminate the notes from the bound volume. This, of couse, was done.

No oral argument was ever allowed on the presentation of a petition for a writ of *certiorari*. Until 1925 the petitions were presented by a member of the Bar, who was usually a Washingtonian acting on behalf of out-of-town counsel. Since then the petitions have been filed with the Clerk and distributed by him to the Justices without oral statement.

For the purpose of impressing the Court with the *importance* of his cases in order thus to bring them within at least one of the reviewable classes, a disappointed suitor, who had been unsuccessful in three Circuit Courts of Appeals—each case involving the identical issue of recovering tariff duties—filed three separate petitions for writs of *certiorari*. On the return day when the Chief Justice asked for motions to be presented, three eminent members of the Bar solemnly rose, one after another, each asking leave to present a petition for a writ of *certiorari* to his respective Circuit Court of Appeals.

The petition in each case was received for consideration, but notwithstanding this impressive presentment, on the following Monday all three were included in the list—which in those days was read at length by the Chief Justice—that began with the words: "In the following cases," and after enumeration of the cases, ended with the ominous declaration: "The petitions for writs of *certiorari* are severally denied."

That list is no longer read in open Court. After the written opinions have been delivered, however, the Chief Justice remarks:

"The other orders of the Court will not be orally an-

111

nounced, but are on a list certified by the Chief Justice and delivered to the Clerk."

Immediately that list is posted in the Bar Conference Room on the main floor. Here every Monday morning a group of attorneys assemble to ascertain the fate of their respective petitions. An average of between 80 and 90 per cent are doomed to disappointment; yet few are surprised. In fact, as a general rule, the only ones surprised are those whose petitions have been granted.

During the past forty years this question has been propounded to me probably several hundred times:

"What proportion of petitions for *certiorari* are granted as against those that are denied?"

My answer usually began with: "Tell me how long is a piece of string and your question will be answered."

There is no set rule according to which the question can be answered. If the case involved is one construing a Federal Statute affecting the nation at large, the chances are probably 90 to 10 that the petition will be granted. They may be even more than that if, as often is the case, the Attorney General files the petition, or does not oppose it.

If there have been diverse decisions of two or more Circuit Courts of Appeals on the same issue, the Supreme Court generally grants the petition in one of the cases, and sometimes in both, in order to determine for future cases, as well as in those instant, what the law actually is in regard to the particular legal problems involved.

If the case does not fall within one of the foregoing classes, but if it has been decided in the Court below by a divided Court—especially if the judgment of the Lower Court was reversed so that the members of all the courts below have evenly split in their opinions—the petitioner has a right to some degree of optimism as to what the action of the Supreme Court will be. If, however, the petitioner was unsuccessful in both Courts below, and the latest opinion was unanimous, he has very little chance of seeing the title of his

OLIVER WENDELL HOLMES

HENRY B. BROWN

EDWARD D. WHITE

case under the heading—"Granted," on the list certified by the Chief Justice and handed to the Clerk.

It has been related above that Chief Justice Hughes told the American Law Institute at their meeting in May, 1937, that about 20 per cent of the petitions filed in the 1936 term were granted. This was close to the usual percentage, but even that cannot be taken as a general guide. It is what is known in statistics as a "loaded" result, based on a combination and average of what happens in all the various classes enumerated in my attempted analysis as above set forth.

Whether or not this attempt on my part will be as successful an exposition of the subject matter as was that of St. Paul in regard to Christianity, it is still my hope that those who read it will agree that defeated suitors in the lower Courts, who have the right to file their petitions for review by the process of *certiorari*, are afforded every opportunity to do so. In all cases they receive fair and proper consideration, and they have no ground of complaint on the lack of ample opportunity to present their pleas for redress to the Supreme Court of the United States.

Chapter XI

ARGUING AT THE SUPREME COURT BAR

MANY TIMES during my stay, official and unofficial, in Washington, my opinion has been asked orally and by letter as to who would be the best lawyer to present a case at the Bar of the Supreme Court of the United States. Generally my responses to such questions have begun—

"Modesty forbids a truthful answer to your question—"
but have continued with the further statement that, in my opinion, the question cannot be answered in the sense that it is usually asked. Such inquiries usually are designed to learn what advocate at the time so has the ear of the Court by reason of its confidence in him and in his arguments that his client's case will be favorably affected because of the advocate's personality.

The Supreme Court of the United States is not influenced by the prominence or standing of counsel presenting the cases of their clients. This does not mean that some lawyers are not better advocates than others, but it does mean that no lawyer of average ability, who thoroughly understands the facts of his case and the law applicable thereto, is handicapped by the mere fact that he is not so well known and outstanding a member of the Bar as others who have appeared oftener in the Court and who have a larger practice.

Many cases are presented where counsel on both sides are of high standing. If that element is to be considered then the odds are even. Many cases also have been brought before the Court in which hitherto unknown members of the Bar have successfully contended against recognized leaders of it.

To my knowledge a case was decided in favor of the client of a lawyer who was making his first appearance before the Court in a major matter, and who was opposed by the highest legal officers of the United States. That case was won, in my opinion, because it was presented by an advocate so thoroughly familiar with the facts and the law involved, that he was able to answer every one of the many questions asked by members of the Court.

It has been my rule to advise attorneys to argue their own cases, and above all to make their own statements of facts, even if they consider it advisable to have other counsel, for any reason whatever, make the closing arguments. It is not unusual when listening to an argument by eminent counsel, who has been retained on account of his high standing at the Bar, but who has not heretofore been connected with the particular case under argument, to observe that he becomes more or less embarrassed by questions asked by members of the Court. Because of his unfamiliarity with the intimate history of the case, such eminent counsel is unable to answer these questions. The old adage —"he who hesitates is lost," may well be paraphrased: "If his lawyer hesitates, the client may be lost."

Once a lawyer friend of mine, who was not only thoroughly familiar with all the intricacies of a complicated case, but also fully able to argue it, was forced by his client to allow the case in which he had been attorney from the start, to be presented by a very eminent member of the Bar, simply for the purpose of having a noted advocate present it.

Listening to the argument, it was rather pathetic to watch my friend as the new counsel, who had superseded him and who was an able veteran in law, but a novice in this particular case, floundered about as he attempted to answer questions put to him by the Court. When the argument was done, in reply to my inquiry as to how he felt while it was being carried on, my friend said:

"Just as any father would feel while some one was

115

strangling his pet baby, and he was tied in a chair and unable to do anything to save the baby."

Attorneys, especially younger ones, should study their cases from every angle and become perfectly familiar with all the facts and the law applicable thereto *pro* and *con*. Then when the cases do reach the Supreme Court of the United States, they should present them without fear of being over-awed, or any suspicion that the Court will be influenced by the eminence of any counsel their opponents may have enlisted in their service.

One thing of which all attorneys and their clients can be sure is that, no matter by whom cases may be presented, or who may appear against them—or whether the cases are submitted by either or both parties on the briefs without argument—when those cases actually reach the conference room of the Court, they will be considered and decided on their merits and not on the relative professional standing of counsel presenting them.

Chapter XII

ADMISSION TO THE SUPREME COURT BAR

D URING THE past forty years the Court has made
several changes in its rules on admission of members
to its Bar. There are no specific tests of eligibility to practice so far as education and capability are concerned. The
basic requirements are that the candidate must have been
a member of the Bar of the highest Court of one of the States
or Territories of the United States for at least three years;
that he must be in good standing at the time of his admission; and that he take an oath, to be administered by the
Clerk, that he will conform to the rules of the Court and
support the Constitution of the United States.

In December, 1902, when I became the Reporter, and for
many years thereafter, any member of the Bar of the Court
could move the Court to admit any person who fulfilled
these requirements; and on this member's mere say-so, his
candidate became a member of the Bar of the highest Court
in the world.

The knowledge of my constant attendance at the Court
was availed of by many out-of-town friends to ask me to
move the admission of their friends for membership at the
Bar of the Court. As a usual thing it was a pleasure for me
to comply with these requests.

It frequently happened also that Senators and Representatives would bring their friends to the Court Room, introduce
them to me and ask me to move their admission to the Bar,
as their own presence was required in their respective legislative chambers. During my Reportership the rules remained unchanged and in those fourteen years undoubtedly

more than 100 attorneys were added, on my motion, to the roll of attorneys of the Supreme Court of the United States.

More than once there were several simultaneous admissions. On one occasion a letter from a friend in New York was presented to me at my office, asking me to move the admission of the bearer. On my agreeing to do so, this gentleman told me that his son was with him and would like to be moved in also. Arriving at the Court a few minutes before twelve noon, he met me in the lobby and said that his wife and daughter, who also were members of the New York Bar, had made up their minds the night before that they, too, would like to be members of the Supreme Court Bar, and had come to Washington for that purpose.

More than once husband and wife, father and daughter, or son, and mother and daughter have been simultaneously admitted; but this was probably the only time that father, mother, son and daughter simultaneously became members of the Bar of the Supreme Court of the United States. When I returned to my seat, a page boy handed me one of the little inter-Court memorandum slips on which these words were written:

"Does the Clerk give you family rates for admissions? Brewer, J."

My response was: "No, but he ought to."

This casual method of moving admissions to the Bar sometimes caused embarrassment. Once it was found that a member of the Bar, who moved the admission of a friend, had not been informed of his friend's disbarment from the State Court of which he was supposed to be a member. The friend, therefore, was not entitled to admission to the Bar of the Supreme Court of the United States, or to any other bar for that matter, except perhaps for bibulous purposes. Fortunately this disqualification did not apply to any of my nominees for admission.

In 1925 the rule for admission was modified to the effect that no one could be "moved in" until he had filed with the

Clerk a certificate that he had been a member of the Bar of the highest Court of his State for more than three years and *was still in good standing*. Also the mover was required to declare how long he had known the candidate, and that he "vouched for him." This created a new situation as to the admission of a friend of a friend.

Often a mover would be heard to acknowledge that he had known the candidate for only a few days, but that the candidate was strongly endorsed by a person in whom the mover had confidence, and he would vouch for him. On the day my son, Henry, was to be admitted we called on Chief Justice Hughes in the Robing Room before the opening of the Court. Henry was introduced to the Chief Justice, who, when he heard me say that my "vouching" was based on having known Henry all his life, observed:

"Perhaps you had better say *but* you vouch for him."

In 1936 the rules on admission to the Bar of the Supreme Court were again changed; and now applying for membership in that Bar is somewhat similar in procedure to applying for membership in many social clubs.

The candidate signs an application giving details of his life and professional career. This must be accompanied not only by the Clerk's certificate as to the candidate's membership for more than three years in the Bar of the highest Court of his State and his present good standing therein, but also by letters from two members of the Bar of that State, who are not related to him and who vouch for his good character and eligibility.

After these "credentials," as they are called, have been filed, a motion may be made by any member of the Bar of the Supreme Court for the admission of the candidate. The mover gives the name of the candidate and of the State, and adds that he has personally examined the credentials in the Clerk's office, has found them in order, and that he is satisfied his candidate has the necessary qualifications.

Until the new rules came into effect when one mover had

more than one candidate it was necessary to move the admission of each separately and to set forth all the details in each statement. This took a great deal of time when there were numerous candidates for admission. On the day the Court held its first session in the new Court building, there were more than 100 candidates and it took more than an hour to complete the ceremony.

Now all candidates of one mover can be moved in together, which greatly shortens the proceeding. Before the later rules were adopted, the candidate had to be described as—"a member of the *Bar* of the highest Court of the State of"—; and in about twenty-five per cent of the instances, the mover, omitting the words "of the Bar," would say that his candidate was "a member of the highest Court of the State of"—thus breveting his candidate with a judgeship to which he had no title.

It fell to my lot once to move the admission of "the Honorable Charles F. Brown, a member of the highest Court of the State of New York;" and then to add, to show there was no mistake—"a former member of the Court of Appeals of that State." Judge Brown was a man much older than myself, and had been a roommate at Yale College of my one-time senior partner, Judge Holt. After retiring from the Court of Appeals at the age of seventy, by reason of the requirement of the State Constitution, Judge Brown resumed the practice of law, and was about to argue his first case before the Supreme Court of the United States.

My friend the Clerk says that it would be too difficult a task to go through the records of thirty-eight years to ascertain how many members of the Bar were sponsored by me; yet as several were moved in at every term, he is sure that I have moved in more than one hundred, and more than any other member of the Bar.

For a long time, that very brilliant member of the Bar, James M. Beck, claimed the distinction of having moved in more members than anyone else because, during his

THE SUPREME COURT OF THE UNITED STATES
1911

Standing, left to right: Willis Van Devanter; Horace Harmon Lurton; Charles Evans Hughes; Joseph Rucker Lamar.

Seated: Oliver Wendell Holmes; John Marshall Harlan; Chief Justice Edward Douglass White; Joseph McKenna; William Rufus Day.

MAHLON PITNEY

WILLIAM R. DAY

term of office as Solicitor General, there was a three-day conference in Washington of Attorneys General and Assistant Attorneys General of the States, and during those days he made more than fifty motions for admission to the Bar.

While Mr. Beck may have moved a greater number than have I in a shorter period, my total, during more than a third of a century, has certainly exceeded his total. On this subject the genial and efficient Clerk of the Court, Charles Elmore Cropley, said:

"Undoubtedly Mr. Butler holds the 'endurance record' in respect to admissions to the Bar of the Court, and by the same token has all the greater responsibility on his shoulders."

Fortunately none of my chickens have ever "come home to roost" in the sense in which that expression is often used.

For many years the Court met at twelve o'clock noon and sat continuously until four o'clock. This procedure continued until a short time before my appointment as Reporter. There was a space back of the Bench wide enough to accommodate small tables on which the messengers of the Justices would serve them luncheon from the kitchen of the Senate Restaurant. As not more than two Justices usually took luncheon at the same time, there would always be a quorum on the Bench. While the partition between the rear of the Bench and the space in which the luncheon tables stood—it was somewhat in the nature of an altar reredos,— prevented the audience in the Court Room from seeing what was going on behind this screen, the rattle of the knives and forks, and sometimes the directions of the Justices to their messengers could be heard very distinctly.

The Judicial Code requires at least six members to constitute a quorum. Shortly before my appearance on the scene a case was being argued before only seven Justices, as inclement weather had kept two of them at home. During the argument two of the Justices retired behind the screen for luncheon. Mr. Frank Hackett, who told me the story himself, stopped his argument. Asked by the Chief Justice to proceed, he said:

"If it please your Honor, there does not seem to be a quorum of the Court present."

To this the Chief Justice returned:

"Although you may not see them, Mr. Hackett, there are two Justices present who can hear the argument, and you may proceed."

According to my friend Hackett, a few weeks thereafter the Court announced that they would sit from twelve until two, then take a recess for half an hour, after which they would sit from half past two until half past four. Such was the custom when my Reportership began and it has continued ever since.

There is another story about the institution of the luncheon recess—the truth of which has never been established— to the effect that on one occasion a Justice added to his menu a pint bottle of champagne. When the messenger who acted as waiter attempted to open the champagne, the cork not only popped out, as sometimes happens, but it flew over the screen and landed in the lap of one of the Justices still remaining on the Bench. This story was not told me by Marshal Wright and is not vouched for by me.

The Court has always been very punctual not only in its appearance and in opening the session at exactly twelve o'clock, but also in closing at exactly the time set for adjournment. On several occasions when, owing to bad weather, a quorum of the Court had not arrived at the Robing Room in time to be ushered in at precisely twelve o'clock, my response to suggestions that the Court was late, would always be:

"Not at all. The Court is not late. The clock is fast."

Speaking of the punctuality of the Court in regard to adjournment, Marshal Wright, my chief source of supply of Court anecdotes, did tell me this story. Chief Justice Fuller was an appointee of President Cleveland. Mr. Cleveland never appeared before the Court but once. That was during his interregnum, and while he was a member of a well-known firm of New York lawyers. His name appeared on the upper left hand corner of their letterheads as "Counsel."

At his single appearance before the Court, one afternoon, Mr. Cleveland having the last word, while finishing his argument at about two minutes before closing time, looked up at the clock. He remarked to the Court that he noticed it was closing time, but added that he would detain them for only a very few minutes to complete his argument.

Thereupon the Chief Justice, bowing with great courtesy, replied:

"Mr. Cleveland, we will hear you tomorrow morning."

It takes more than an ex-President to have the Court sit over-time, even if that ex-President has himself appointed the presiding officer.

Chapter XIII

SOCIAL ETIQUETTE OF THE SUPREME COURT

ON ACCOUNT of the death of Mrs. Fuller in July, 1907, Chief Justice Fuller asked to be excused from attending the next annual dinner given by the President to the Chief Justice and members of the Supreme Court. The regular list of guests for this function up to that time not only included, as it still does, the Attorney General of the United States, but also until then, the Speaker of the House of Representatives. The officers of the Court were not invited, although on several occasions Mrs. Butler and I were among the guests bidden to the musicale which usually followed the dinner.

On the afternoon of the day following the dinner of 1908, I was horseback riding in Potomac Park with Attorney General Moody, later Associate Justice Moody, who said to me:

"Butler, let me tell you something that happened at the White House dinner last night."

It seems that at about the middle of the dinner, President Theodore Roosevelt called the attention of Justice Brewer to the fact that Joseph G. Cannon, the Speaker of the House of Representatives, was not present. The President explained the Speaker's absence as follows:

At three o'clock that afternoon, William Loeb, the President's Secretary, told the President that Speaker Cannon was awaiting an answer on the telephone to the Speaker's inquiry as to who was to escort Mrs. Roosevelt to the dinner table. The President instructed Mr. Loeb to say that as this dinner was in honor of the Supreme Court, Mr. Justice

124

Harlan, the senior Justice, in the unavoidable absence of the Chief Justice, would escort Mrs. Roosevelt.

Loeb returned to the President with the further message from the Speaker to the effect that, while he was always ready to yield to the Chief Justice, he did not think that the Speaker of the House of Representatives should yield to an Associate Justice and, therefore, asked to be excused. As Attorney General Moody related the incident to me, the President's reply was:

"All right, Loeb, tell Uncle Joe I appreciate his feelings and, while sorry to miss him, he can be excused and I'll give him another dinner all for himself."

And that is the reason the Speaker's Dinner has been one of the official White House functions ever since that night.

Joseph G. Cannon was a remarkable man individually and as Speaker of the House. Numerous interesting stories could be collected and told about him. He was called "Chief of the Clan of the Plain People," and many were surprised at his attitude in the incident just narrated. He would sit anywhere at anybody's table, if it was a private affair, but if his location involved the relative rank of himself and others in officialdom, he insisted that, as head of the Legislative Branch of the Government, he out-ranked everybody except the President, Vice President and Chief Justice—the heads of the other two great departments of our National Government. In my opinion Speaker Cannon was absolutely right in this feeling.

Uncle Joe, as he was affectionately called, was a very loyal supporter of Theodore Roosevelt, although he did not always agree with him; and he had a real affection for the President. Once while dining at our house, he expressed his admiration for the President and then went on to say:

"Teddy was not always right—in fact, he made a good many mistakes—but he had the remarkable faculty of finding out himself when he made a mistake before anyone else did, and immediately 'lighting a new fire,' thus distracting the attention of the public and effacing or neutralizing the results of his previous error of judgment."

Uncle Joe was indeed a picturesque character and his departure from public life left a great gap in all the various Washington circles in which he moved. We all owe him a debt of gratitude for his work as Chairman of the Lincoln Memorial Committee and for standing by his guns in confining the Memorial to Lincoln and to Lincoln alone. As he said more than once, there was nobody else and nothing else big enough to go with, or in, a monument erected to Abraham Lincoln.

Probably the most remarkable event connected with what might be called the "right of way," rather than individual precedence, of different groups at official functions, happened at the White House Judiciary Reception of 1907. Theodore Roosevelt was President; Elihu Root was Secretary of State; Melville W. Fuller was Chief Justice; Mr. Justice Harlan was Senior Justice; Captain, later Major General, Charles L. MacCawley, of the Marine Corps of the United States Navy, was Chief Aide at the White House. All these figured in the episode about to be related.

To my everlasting regret, my unavoidable absence in New York prevented me from attending the reception. However, Mrs. Butler was present—Justice and Mrs. Harlan had taken her under their protective wing—and from her came my knowledge of the details of this occurrence.

Resident diplomats attending receptions at the White House *in a body* are always (and properly so) accorded the right of way over other bodies of visitors. The same custom still obtains at the Diplomatic Reception, which is the first of the annual series of White House receptions, and generally opens the official social season.

At these functions the Diplomatic Corps come attired in full court regalia, assemble in a designated room, and then pass by the President and the receiving line in the order prescribed by the Vienna Protocol of 1815. At other White House receptions the diplomats do not come in a body, or in diplomatic dress, but arrive whenever convenient and are ushered to "the front of the line." The Judiciary Reception of 1907, so far as my knowledge is concerned, was the only exception to this very sensible course of procedure.

According to the story as told to me, Secretary Root, on some occasion when they met casually after the Diplomatic and before the Judiciary Reception of 1907, asked the Dean of the Diplomatic Corps if it would not be a pleasant change to have the members of the corps attend the other receptions, as well as the Diplomatic, in their official regalia. The Dean responded that if it were so desired, so it would be done,—a sort of "we strive to please" answer and a diplomatic one.

Nothing more seems to have been said or done until the night of the next reception, which happened to be the "Judiciary Reception." To the great surprise—or rather to the horror—of all officialdom, the entire Diplomatic Corps arrived in full regalia and, assembling as usual in true Vienna Protocol order, the Dean of the Corps informed one of the aides that they were ready to enter. There they were, not as private guests as heretofore had been the case, but as the Diplomatic Corps at the invitation of the Secretary of State, and they expected to lead the procession.

Here indeed was a pretty how-to-do. At the Judiciary Receptions, the Chief Justice of the Supreme Court of the United States always had and, except on this occasion, always has led the way. This time, however, after the fanfare had announced the presence of President and Mrs. Theodore Roosevelt, and the Chief Justice had offered his arm to Mrs. Fuller and was about to proceed, suddenly Captain MacCawley appeared before them and said:

"Mr. Chief Justice, the Secretary of State asks me to tell you that the Diplomatic Corps will precede you tonight."

It was too late for anybody to say anything. The Diplo-

127

matic Corps was already passing the group assembled around the Chief Justice. According to Mrs. Butler's account, the Chief Justice protested to the aides. Mrs. Fuller wanted everybody to go downstairs, call for their carriages and go home. Justice Harlan wanted to do something more or less desperate—to judge from what he told me. To hang, draw and quarter the aide, he said, would have been too moderate a punishment. Justice Harlan insisted that the aide had actually "assaulted" the Chief Justice, because he touched the lapel of his coat as he delivered the message from Secretary Root. Subsequently Justice Harlan added the adverb "violently" to his description of the "assault."

For all that, the Court went "through the line" though most of its members left the White House at an early hour. Next morning the Chief Justice and Senior Associate Justice Harlan called on the President. The whole matter was explained in as satisfactory a manner as possible. Secretary Root assured the Chief Justice and the Senior Justice that such an incident could not happen again. Members of the Diplomatic Corps, he said, much preferred attending all receptions, except the Diplomatic Reception, in ordinary evening dress, at their convenience, and would be glad to be relieved of the necessity of donning court dress and assembling at a set hour, which they were obliged to do at the New Year's and the Diplomatic Receptions. And so the storm blew over.

It afforded Mr. Justice Harlan, however, a great deal of joy to tell how "that little whippersnapper of a lieutenant dashed into the room and actually and violently assaulted the Chief Justice of the United States in order to prevent him from leading the line to greet the President and Mrs. Roosevelt at the Judiciary Reception."

At about this time cards for the White House receptions were changed. As told to me, the Dean of the Diplomatic Corps advised the Secretary of State that because the members of his corps represented sovereigns, they could not be

WILLIAM HOWARD TAFT

JAMES C. MCREYNOLDS

1535 EYE STREET

The Washington Residence of the Author
1902–1933

THE LIBRARY AT 1535 EYE STREET WITH THE AUTHOR AT HIS DESK

invited to meet anyone beneath the rank of a sovereign. Therefore, as there were no sovereigns to meet, the invitations to White House receptions were changed to read that, The President of the United States and Mrs. (as the name might be) invite you to a reception (at a certain time) "in honor of the Chief Justice,"—instead of "to meet the Chief Justice," as had been the custom previously.

CHAPTER XIV

MEMORIAL TRIBUTES

EVEN AS Mr. Justice Nelson of the Supreme Court, participated in paying the last respects to my grandfather by presiding at the memorial meeting held in New York City, after his remains had been brought back from Paris where he had died in November, 1858, so my grandfather and members of his family have participated in paying the last honors to members of the Supreme Court of the United States as they passed to their final resting places.

After the death of Chief Justice Marshall my grandfather presented to the Supreme Court of the United States the memorial resolutions adopted by Bar Associations, and had them entered in the minutes of the Court.

At the memorial meeting of the Bar of the City of New York in honor of Chief Justice Waite, who died suddenly in March 1888, my father made one of the principal addresses, in which he remarked:

"It might be truly said that never since its organization, nearly one hundred years ago, has the Supreme Court of the United States been so near the thought, the sympathy, and the heart of the American people as during the ten days just past."

Continuing his address my father quoted Mr. Pinckney's characterization of the Supreme Court in his famous argument in *McCulloch* vs. *Maryland* * as being "distinguished by all that can give to judicature a title to reverency; as a more than an amphictyonic council," as illustrating the reverence of the Court which has never been disconnected from

* (17 U.S. 316.)

130

the great names of Marshall, Story and their associates whom Pinckney addressed when he made that statement. In closing my father said:

"Chief Justice Marshall stands with us as to constitutional law as Lord Mansfield stands as to commercial law, and we are, perhaps, to make the great constitutional Chief Justice a pattern and exemplar of the judicial fitness and fame which should attach to his successors and of the qualifications required for fit succession.

"But it is the Supreme Court as a whole which is the conservator and interpreter of our constitutional rights, and it is not so much its highest honor to have been and to be presided over, or to include men of unmatched abilities, if indeed that could be claimed, but that as a Court it has steadily been true to the trust and equal to the trust with which the people have invested it; that it has kept pace with the growing needs of the country, and has itself grown in wisdom with the nation's growth in wealth and power.

"Mr. O'Conor has been reported in the Court of Appeals, as happily illustrating this fact when he said 'that Admiralty jurisdiction could exist without tidewater or saltwater was an idea too novel for even the great mind of Chief Justice Marshall, but at last judicial wisdom, sharpened and impelled by strong necessity, cast aside these immaterial incidents and, looking at the substance of the thing, found in the Constitution a government for our great rivers and inland seas.'

"It was reserved for the Court in which Chief Justice Taney presided to announce the final establishment of this enlarged grant of power which Marshall and Story had denied, and for the Court in which Chief Justice Waite has just ceased to preside to give it even wider scope in aid of the commercial interests of the nation.

"Chief Justice Waite was in sympathy with an enlightened progress and a wise exercise and maintenance of the judicial power. He was no doctrinaire or extremist. He was courageous, but not too bold. He was neither scared,

131

on the one side, by usurping and overreaching Acts of Congress; nor, on the other side by the cry of 'judge-made law,' so often raised as an obstacle on the way of a needed exercise of the judicial power.

"To him we may properly apply the words of the Court, in its tribute to Chief Justice Chase: 'He died with the armor of duty on, wearing the honors of a great and conscientious magistrate.' Faithful to the last, the end came as rest comes to a weary laborer at the close of a long, hard day's work.

"There seemed to me something very touching and pathetic, and almost consoling, in the brief notice, on the day of his death, of the manner of his dying. In the early morning, after a restless night, he is reported to have said to his sole attendant: 'I feel better, and will go to sleep'—then turned his head on the pillow and slept. This was the serene, quiet, silent ending of a life which had been filled with so much activity and crowned with so much honor, and which, so long as it lasted, stood as the embodiment of the highest of all the functions on whose fit discharge the fabric of society rests—this life went out at a touch as light as that of

> " 'Summer's evening latest sigh
> Which shuts the rose.'

"To such a death we may well apply the wealth of imagery of the English poetess in lines whose beauty is not marred by their familiar use:

> " 'So fades a summer cloud away;
> So sinks a gale when storms are o'er;
> So gently shuts the eye of day;
> So dies a wave along the shore.'

"And over this sleeping form, borne to its rest with all the honors a nation pays to those who have served it best, what better inscription can we write than that so often found in the Roman Catacombs on the tombs of the early Christian martyrs—

" 'IN PACE DOMINI DORMIT' "

During my Reportership the records of the Court will show my official attendance at funerals of several of the Justices who died while they were still on the Bench.

Chief Justice Fuller died suddenly at his summer home in Sorrento, Maine, just opposite Bar Harbor, on July 4, 1910, during vacation of the Court. We were at Round Oak, Yonkers, at the time. Mr. Justice Harlan, the Senior Justice, who thus became also the Presiding Justice, was at his summer home at Murray Bay, Canada. He telegraphed, asking me as an officer of the Court to attend the services at Sorrento and Chicago, and to write him a full account thereof, which was done.

Unfortunately the Bar Harbor Express, due in ample time for the services, was delayed by a freight train wreck. In consequence several of us bound on the same sad errand were unable to reach Sorrento until the cortège was on its way to the train to which a special car for the funeral party to Chicago was attached. The then Reverend Dr. James E. Freeman, now Bishop Freeman of Washington, a neighbor and very dear friend of the Chief Justice, conducted the services both at Sorrento and at Chicago, where the interment took place.

"Thrice within a period of nine months, has the hand of death reached forth, has its finger pointed to a member of the Supreme Court of the United States."

Thus commenced a "Memorial Note: Melville Weston Fuller: David Josiah Brewer," which was written by myself at the request of the Editors of the American Journal of International Law for the issue of October, 1910.

Mr. Justice Peckham died on October 24, 1909, at his home in Altamont, near Albany, New York. The funeral services were held in Albany and were attended by the entire Court, members and officers. Mr. Justice Brewer died suddenly on Sunday morning, March 28, 1910, at his home in Washington. This was a great shock, especially to those, who like myself, had seen and talked with him on Saturday evening. Memorial Resolutions adopted at a meeting of the Supreme Court Bar were presented to the Court on the last day of the 1909 Term, and accepted by the Chief Justice in words hereafter to be alluded to.

The Memorial Note referred only to the Chief Justice and Mr. Justice Brewer because of their participation in matters and cases before Commissions and Courts involving questions of international law, and as such of interest to readers of the Journal. Also they both were Vice Presidents and members of the Executive Council, and had shared the activities of the American Society of International Law, of which the Journal is the official organ.

As a charter member of the society, then a member and later chairman of its Executive Council from the date of its organization, it was a pleasure for me to comply with this request of the Editors of the American Journal of International Law. The Memorial Note is too long to he included here in full, and only passing reference can be made to the numerous questions involving problems of international law which were treated by these two members of the Court. Especially notable was their effort in the Venezuela-Great Britain Boundary dispute, which elicited from President Cleveland and Secretary of State Olney in 1895 the famous redeclaration of the Monroe Doctrine, and the establishment of an international boundary commission on which the Chief Justice and Mr. Justice Brewer served. The result was a final determination—satisfactory to and accepted by all interested parties—of a boundary which had periodically threatened the amicable relations of three countries for more than half a century.

134

After reviewing other national and international judicial activities of these two eminent men, the Memorial continues:

"These are but a paltry few of the cases decided and opinions delivered by these two jurists. It would involve an examination of between seventy-five and one hundred volumes of reports to review them all: the few that are cited have been selected to show what broad subjects they were called upon to consider and how they were able to meet the great questions involved as they arose.

"But there is another phase of the lives of these men which deeply impressed all who knew them intimately. There was a divinely human side to each. The hand that could without a tremor sign the decree that settled the fate in the pending controversy of man or State or nation could yet reach forth and hand a cup of cold water to the least who needed it. There was intellect, but there was heart also; each was a consistent and zealous Christian, in private life as well as in the Church; and each held high office in his own denomination. Each recognized his duty to his fellow man and did his best to fulfill it.

"Nothwithstanding their arduous labors on the bench each found some time to devote to the affairs of their fellow men. The Chief Justice gave a full quota of attention to the Smithsonian Institution, of which he was the Chancellor, and to the Peabody Education Fund, of which he was a trustee; Mr. Justice Brewer for years acted as president of the charity organization of our capital city. Each could well and truly have said for himself—

> " 'I live for those who love me
> Who know me well and true,
> For the Heaven that smiles above me
> To receive my spirit too.
> For the wrong that need resistance,
> For the right that need assistance,
> For the future in the distance,
> For the good that I may do.'

135

Of all the utterances of Chief Justice Fuller, and they were many, and were pronounced in cases of far-reaching importance and involving great principles, none have left a deeper impression on me than those uttered at the last session of the 1909 Term of the Court, over which he had presided for twenty-two years, when with heart-felt and throbbing emotion, he responded to the remarks of Attorney General Wickersham on presenting the resolutions of the Bar on the death of Mr. Justice Brewer.

As the Memorial says in reference to this occasion:

"The Chief Justice voiced the sentiments of all those who knew Justice Brewer intimately when he declared 'that it was not his magnificent judicial labors, but the ineffable sweetness of his disposition that chiefly impressed itself upon us.'

"Surely the same words can apply to the Chief Justice himself, and there can be no words more fitting, as to both of its subjects with which to close this article than those in which, on the same occasion, the survivor paid a beautiful and affectionate farewell to the loved brother and colleague who had preceded him. 'It has been my sad duty,' he said further in response to the Attorney General, 'to accept for the Court tributes of the Bar in memory of the many members of this tribunal who have passed to their reward. As our Brother Brewer joins the great procession, there pass before me the forms of Matthews and Miller, of Field and Bradley and Lamar and Blatchford, of Jackson and Gray and of Peckham, whose works follow them now that they rest from their labors. They were all men of marked ability, of untiring industry, and of intense devotion to duty, but they were not alike. They differed "as one star differs from another star in glory." Their names will remain illustrious in the annals of jurisprudence. And now we are called on to deplore the departure of one of the most lovable of them all.

" 'He died suddenly, but not the unprepared death from which we pray to be delivered. When the unexpected intelligence was conveyed to me, I could not but think of Mrs. Barbauld's poem on Life, and seemed to hear our dear friend exclaim:

> " 'Life! we've been long together,
> Through pleasant and through cloudy weather;
> 'Tis hard to part when friends are dear;
> Perhaps 'twill cost a sigh, a tear;
> Then steal away, give little warning,
> Choose thine own time;
> Say not good night, but in some brighter clime
> Bid me Good morning.' "

" 'Even so'—and in the same affectionate spirit let us say of them both—*They rest from their labors and their works do follow them.*' "

After the death of Mr. Justice Blatchford in July 1893, my father wrote a letter of appreciation of that jurist's ability and faithfulness to duty, which was published in the New York *Evening Post.*

When Mr. Justice Brown, who retired in 1906, died in September 1913, *The Green Bag,* a well-known legal magazine, in its issue of November of that year published an obituary article about him which was written by me at its request.

The respective Presidents of the American, New York City, and District of Columbia Bar Associations appointed me to act as a member—in one case as chairman—of the committees of their respective organizations to attend the funeral services of Chief Justice Taft (retired), who died at Washington in March 1930. A similar duty was performed as a member of more than one of such committees to attend the funeral services of Mr. Justice Holmes.

CHAPTER XV

CENTENNIAL AND SESQUICENTENNIAL CELEBRATIONS

IT WAS surely an unintentional oversight on the part of President Franklin D. Roosevelt when, in his address at the opening of the New York World's Fair, April 30, 1939, the sesquicentennial anniversary of the inauguration of President Washington, Mr. Roosevelt said that all sesquicentennials of the initial events in the establishment of our National Government were past and had been celebrated.

He enumerated the Ratification of the Federal Constitution, the First Meeting of Congress, and the event then being celebrated. He omitted, however, to mention the sesquicentennial of the first meeting of the Supreme Court of the United States in the Royal Exchange Building in New York City on February 1, 1790. The centennial anniversary of this occasion was celebrated in New York on February 4, 1890; and the sesquicentennial was celebrated on February 1, 1940 by very simple ceremonies in the Court Room at Washington, and elsewhere, as is told hereafter.

During the year 1889, at the annual meetings of the New York State, City, and American Bar Associations, committees were appointed to arrange for a centennial celebration of the most historic event in the history of the Judiciary of our country. The American Bar Association met that year in Chicago. David Dudley Field, one of the most prominent members of the New York Bar, was its President. He was then eighty-seven years of age. Notwithstanding the disparity of our years, a warm friendship existed between Mr. Field and myself. He had taken me to the Chicago meeting not only as his guest, but also as his personal secretary, to help him in the discharge of his presidential duties.

During the session, and on my motion, a resolution was adopted for the appointment of a committee of the Association to co-operate with the other Associations in the celebration of the Judiciary Centennial. Mr. Field was chairman of this committee and the nine other members were: Lyman Trumbull, Illinois; Thomas J. Semmes, Louisiana; William C. Endicott, Massachusetts; Edward J. Phelps, Vermont; J. Randolph Tucker, Virginia; Henry Hitchcock, Missouri; Cortlandt Parker, New Jersey; Francis Rawle, Pennsylvania; Henry Wise Garnett, District of Columbia, and Charles Henry Butler, New York, who was appointed Secretary of the Committee.

At the meeting of the American Bar Association in 1890, the report of this committee showed that it was merged into one large committee, which consisted of members of the three different Bar Associations, co-operating in this respect.

As David Dudley Field's brother, Stephen J. Field, was then Senior Associate Justice of the Supreme Court, the former was, of course, greatly interested in the celebration, and took an active part in the arrangements for it. One result of his activities was that at the morning session, three of the orators, Messrs. Hitchcock, Semmes and Phelps, had not only been Presidents of the American Bar Association, but also were members of the committee of which David Dudley Field was chairman. The fourth orator, William Allen Butler, was not a member of that committee, but was an ex-President of the Association. Also he had been chairman of the "Plan and Scope" subcommittee whose adopted recommendations were that the celebration "should be characterized by simplicity and dignity, and so arranged as to bring into prominence before the nation the distinctive character and functions of the Court as a co-ordinate branch of the Government, and to exhibit its influence in our national history; and also to give an opportunity, as far as practicable, for a manifestation of the respect and esteem in which the members of the Court, as now constituted, are held by our citizens."

The report also made a recommendation for a suitable memorial volume of all that transpired during the celebration. The various committees were consolidated into the

·1790 ≋ 1890·

≋ Centennial Celebration ≋

OF THE ORGANIZATION OF THE

··Federal · Judiciary··

Commemorative Literary Exercises

Metropolitan Opera House

New York City

Tuesday morning, February 4th, 1890

Centennial Judiciary Committee, and increased to 112 members. Mr.—later Judge—William H. Arnoux, President of the New York State Bar Association, became chairman of the General Committee. Former President Grover Cleveland was chairman of the Executive Committee; and various subcommittees were established to attend to the different phases of the celebration.

As Secretary of the Dinner Committee it fell to my lot to have practically entire charge of the material elements of the banquet, which was one of the chief features of the celebration. Fortunately there were separate subcommittees on toasts, menus and the selection of viands and wines. Our committee of three had charge of the arrangement and decoration of the tables and of the seatings at them. The other two members frankly avowed they knew nothing about banquets, and subsequently demonstrated the truthfulness of their avowal; and also of the saying that the most effective committee is a committee of three, one of whom knows something about the matter in hand, one of whom is sick in bed, and the other gone to Europe.

The press devoted much space to the celebration. It was an event of distinctive news value, not only for lawyers but also for the general public, which always, as has been sharply demonstrated in late years, is interested in the existence and the preservation of the Supreme Court of the United States. An editorial of the New York *Times* made special comment on Father's address, which was published in full in the New York *Evening Post*. The group photograph of the Court here reproduced is from a copy autographed by all the members of the Court. It was sent to me through the Marshal, a much appreciated compliment as few copies were distributed in this manner. This photograph now hangs in my son's home in Washington.

The banquet was held in the Lenox Lyceum at the corner of Madison Avenue and Fifty-ninth Street. The Lyceum was owned by John D. Crimmins, a man high in New York City politics, who gave the committee his assurances—which were scrupulously fulfilled—that everything within the range of possibility would be done to make the banquet the most successful one ever held in New York.

The banquet was served on a double story floor, consisting of one large circular room with a mezzanine gallery for boxes. The only caterer in that part of the city had never

141

handled such a gathering before, but he demonstrated his ability efficiently and satisfactorily by serving a remarkably fine dinner.

In fact some of the diners, who had lately attended the Centennial Dinner of the Washington Inaugural Celebration—a $20.00 one—at the Metropolitan Opera House, under the chairmanship of Mr. Ward McAllister, declared that our $10.00 dinner was the better of the two. Not having had thirty dollars at the time to pay for two dinners, it is not possible for me to pass judgment on the relative merits of the two repasts; but there is no reason for me to contradict the favorable verdict of those who did have the wherewithal to attend both dinners and were thus enabled to express their opinion.

In respect to the cloakroom accommodations—a most important feature of any such function—the palm of victory must be awarded to the Lenox Lyceum. That cloakroom was my own idea. It was on the first floor with an opening of about 75 feet. The shelf was formed of a series of wide laundry tables. Behind these tables twenty men and women handled the outer garments of more than 1500 diners and gallery guests. Generally less than one or two minutes were required to deposit or recover a garment.

Placing the seating diagram so that the 840 guests at fifteen tables could be seen by the Chief Justice from the center of the main table, my memory can visualize what he might have seen had his vision been prophetic. The reader may judge for himself from the diagram here reproduced.

Almost directly in front of the Chief Justice, at Seat 18, Table G, was Judge Horace H. Lurton, then a Justice of the Supreme Court of Tennessee, who was soon to become a Circuit Judge of the United States for the Fifth Circuit, and was later to be appointed an Associate Justice of the Supreme Court of the United States by President Taft in 1909. Near Judge Lurton, in Seat 1 at Table D, was William B. Hornblower, a prominent member of the Bar, who was to be

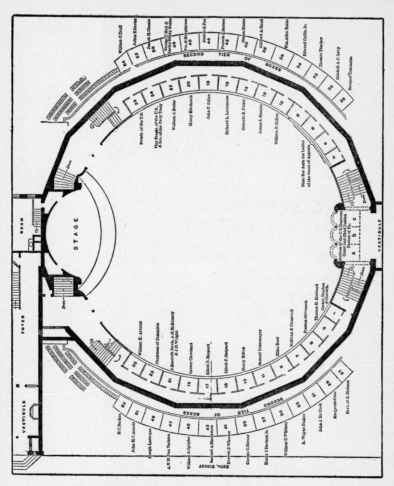

Plan of Lenox Lyceum Gallery Showing
Box Holders at Centennial Celebration Banquet

nominated by President Cleveland as a Justice of the Supreme Court of the United States, to succeed Mr. Justice Blatchford, on this occasion sitting with the Chief Justice at the main table. The confirmation of the appointment of Mr. Hornblower, however, was bitterly and successfully fought by President Cleveland's political enemy, David B. Hill, who had been Governor of the State of New York and was Senator from that State.

A little farther away, at Seat 5, Table B, was Wheeler H. Peckham, whose name was substituted for that of Mr. Hornblower as nominee for the same Associate Justiceship which had been denied Mr. Hornblower. The like hostility defeated the nomination of Mr. Peckham. It made way for the nomination and confirmation of Mr. Justice White, as the result of which New York State was for a while unrepresented on the Supreme Court Bench.

Immediately in front of the Chief Justice, at Seat 7, Table G, was Rufus W. Peckham, of Albany, then a Judge of the New York Court of Appeals. His nomination to succeed Mr. Justice Jackson of the Supreme Court of the United States, met the approval of David B. Hill and was confirmed. Justice Peckham became Chief Justice Fuller's colleague on the Supreme Court Bench in 1895.

At the far end of Table G, directly in front of him, the Chief Justice had he strained his eyes, could have seen the writer, who, about twelve years later was to become the Reporter of the Decisions of the Court and to continue to function as such for fourteen years thereafter.

Had the eye of the Chief Justice wandered as far to the left as possible, he would have seen at Seat 17, Table A, which might well fit the Gospel description of the "lowest room," a young man of twenty-seven years, who was to have a most eventful legal and political history; and who was to be told constantly not only—"Friend, go up higher," but to go higher and higher, and indeed have worship in the presence of those who sat at meat with him.

144

Benjamin N. Cardozo

Louis D. Brandeis

THE SUPREME COURT OF THE UNITED STATES
1933

Standing, left to right: Justice Owen J. Roberts, Justice Pierce Butler, Justice Harlan Fiske Stone,
Justice Benjamin N. Cardozo.

Seated, left to right: Justice Louis D. Brandeis, Justice Willis Van Devanter, Chief Justice

For this young man went on to his State's Governorship, then for a time to an Associate Justiceship of the Supreme Court of the United States, and almost to the White House itself, which he failed to enter only because of a campaign blunder for which he himself was blameless. Then, after a brilliant period of private practice, during which he was chosen by his fellow members of the Bar to fill at one time or another the high offices of President of the American Bar Association, the New York State, the New York County and the New York City Bar Associations and of the American Society of International Law, he was selected for the highest appointive executive office in the country, as Secretary of State. Finally he was exalted to the post of Chief Justice of the United States, which he now [1940] so efficiently and gracefully administers. The young man in Seat 17, Table A was Charles Evans Hughes of New York.

After the celebration was over, and all the bills had been paid, there was a substantial surplus in the hands of the treasurer, which invoked considerable discussion in the Executive Committee as to its proper disposition. It is not unusual after such events for the Committee on Ways and Means to be obliged to devise methods for meeting deficiencies; but in this instance the Committee had been so generously supplied with funds that there was a surplus of more than $8,000 after the payment of all expenses. These expenses included transportation of all the members of the Court and its officers from Washington to New York and back, entertainment of them in New York; the engraving by Tiffany of the banquet menus, rental of the Opera House, and many other items of apparent extravagance, but which were authorized by the Committee only with the knowledge that sufficient funds were on hand to meet all expenditures. Mr. Francis Lynde Stetson, the treasurer, was not only very efficient, but also very meticulous, and carefully scrutinized and audited every item of outlay.

The disposition of the surplus funds was solved by two

resolutions offered by my father. One of these, according to the preface of Carson's "History of the Supreme Court," appropriated $6,000 to procure the publication of that work. Remarkable both from an artistic and an historical standpoint, it was to be known as the "Official Report" of the

Facsimile of Inscription in Copy of Carson's History presented to the Supreme Court Library

celebration, and also as the enduring artistic memorial, as suggested in the report of the Committee on Plan and Scope. The second resolution offered by my father was that the treasurer should transmit the net balance of the surplus to the widow of Mr. Justice Miller, who had died in the meantime. This was done and Mrs. Miller was very grateful for the $2,500 she unexpectedly received.

During the preparations for this celebration many episodes occurred, some of a humorous character, some tragic. The most serious was the tragedy of the fire in the residence of the Secretary of the Navy, Benjamin F. Tracy, on Farragut Square in Washington. It resulted in the death of Mrs. Tracy and in severe injuries to other members of the family. President Harrison, Vice-President Levi P. Morton, and Secretary Tracy, all of whom were to take part in the ceremonies, had to cancel their acceptances immediately.

The program of the morning exercises had to be altered by the omission of the President's address, but that was a simple matter as compared to rearranging the seating of the guests at the banquet. The seating list and diagram of tables were in type, and the changes necessitated by the absence of the highest ranking guests required the relocation of more than one hundred names on the diagram. Printing the list of names and the diagram was part of my duty as Secretary of the Dinner Committee; but the delicate task of seating in their proper places nearly two hundred invited guests, including Federal and State officials, from the President of the United States to municipal judges was under the control of the Executive Committee.

My father and Mr. Stetson, of that Committee, worked with me until late that evening in order to re-seat the guests. Meanwhile a special staff of the Bank Note Company was kept on hand so that the list and diagram could go to press the following day. Thus fortunately the task was duly accomplished.

Always there are people who want to get something for their own advantage out of an event of this nature. Some of these seemed to think their desires could be attained either through me directly or through my influence with other members of the Committee. It was rather a mystery, for instance, why a prominent member of the Bar, who was

147

almost twice my age of thirty, should invite me to luncheon at Delmonico's. The mystery was solved, however, over the coffee, when my host told me he had been overlooked by those who had selected the speakers for the banquet, and he intimated that it was more or less my duty to have this error corrected.

Fortunately the Committee on Toasts had complete charge of that feature of the banquet, so that then, even as now, the favorite indoor sport of "passing the buck" could be resorted to. My anxious host soon found that he had wasted his hospitality, so to speak, on "the desert air." Notwithstanding any further efforts he may have made, his name did not appear on the list of those responding to toasts at the banquet.

A couple of days before the event, a man well known as a "pusher" for a noted champagne distributor, expressed great concern over the fact that his pet brand of that delectable beverage was not listed on the menu. He declared that he was acting for the Chief Justice, who, he said, never drank any other kind of champagne.

When it was explained to him that a special committee of experts had selected the wines and that the menus had already been printed, he offered to pay all expenses for reprinting them. And when he was told that the menus were copperplate engravings by Tiffany & Company, that they had cost more than $2,000, and that it was too late to alter, reprint or amend them, he became almost lachrymose over the fact that the Chief Justice should be deprived of his one and only favorite beverage. Also he refused to be consoled by my assurance that if the Chief Justice expressed a preference for this particular wine, there would be some of it within easy reach to satisfy his thirst. The champagne agent left me with the sad warning that under the circumstances the banquet would be a complete failure. According to my recollection neither the Chief Justice, nor any other guest at the dinner, in any way regretted the Commit-

148

tee's choice of Mumm's Extra Dry and of Irroy Brut to be served with the appropriate courses of the dinner.

The Committee also selected Grand Vin Chateau La Rose for the red wine, and had notified me of the number of cases that would be delivered at the Lenox Lyceum. Calling at the Lyceum with one of my colleagues on the day before the banquet, to check up on sundry matters, we were horrified to find that this delicate product of the vineyards of France, Grand Vin Chateau La Rose—which should be served at the temperature of the room—had been stacked in the refrigerator. This had been done, the custodian said, in order that "it would be real nice and cold" when it was used. The removal of the wine from the refrigerator was quickly made.

THE SESQUICENTENNIAL

Editor's Note:

As EXPLAINED in the Foreword, the author had intended to conclude this chapter with a description of the sesquicentennial, but his illness and death prevented him from doing so. His attendance at the Court on this occasion was his last formal appearance, and it seems fitting to give a brief description of the exercises and of the author's part in them.

On Thursday, February 1, 1940, the one hundred fiftieth anniversary of the assembling of the Supreme Court of the United States was recognized by nation-wide exercises at the graves of deceased Chief Justices and Associate Justices, and by the Court at its regular meeting.

Nine former Justices are buried in and near Washington, and on this memorial day wreaths were placed on their graves by committees appointed by the Bar Association of the District of Columbia, the Women's Bar Association of the District of Columbia, and the Federal Bar Association, with William P. McCracken as general chairman of the Joint Committee of these Associations.

A Joint Committee of the Senate and House of Representatives, of which Congressman Sol Bloom of New York was chairman, sponsored the entire anniversary exercises. Members of the Washington Bar Association committees who were to visit the graves of the Justices assembled at 8:30 in the Senate restaurant for breakfast, after which they visited the former court room of the Supreme Court in the Capitol, and then proceeded in nine groups to the several graves.

The committee appointed to lay a wreath at the tomb of Associate Justice Philip P. Barbour of Virginia, who had been appointed by President Andrew Jackson and who is buried in the Congressional Cemetery in the District of Columbia, was comprised of William Roy Vallance, Chairman, Department of State; Honorable Earl C. Michener, Member of Congress from Michigan; William E. Reese of the General Accounting Office, Charles Henry Butler and George C. Gertman, both of the District of Columbia Bar.

At noon the Court met as usual, and addresses were delivered by Chief Justice Charles Evans Hughes, Attorney General Robert H. Jackson, and Charles A. Beardsley, President of the American Bar Association.

The American Bar Association was represented also by a special committee comprised of Charles Henry Butler, Edgar B. Tolman and Silas H. Strawn.

Just before the Court convened, the author of this volume handed to the Chief Justice, to each Associate Justice present and to several of the Court officers, copies of the Menu of the Banquet at the Centennial Celebration, together with personal letters to each. These letters began:

"The accompanying copies of the Menu of the Banquet at the Centennial Celebration in February, 1890, of the First Session of the Supreme Court of the United States have for the past half century been in my possession as the member of the Centennial Judiciary Committee who was most specifically charged with the arrangements for that feature of the program, as to the success of which the present Chief Justice can take not only judicial, but actual, notice as he was one of the participants therein. On this Sesquicentennial date it would give me great pleasure if you would accept these souvenirs on the pages whereof are portraits of those who then occupied the same positions on, and in connection with, the Court as you do today.

"It is impossible for me to refrain from referring to the pleasant recollections of my fourteen years official connection with the Court or fail to express my sentiments towards the Court and its personnel."

And ended with the same quotation from the Centennial Celebration address of William Allen Butler with which the author concludes this book. Under his signature was the legend:

> Admitted to the Bar of the Supreme Court of the United States, March 18, 1886 on Motion of Joseph H. Choate; Reporter of its Decisions from 1902 to 1916; only survivor of the 112 members of the Centennial Judiciary Committee of 1890; member of Sesquicentennial Committee of 1940.

The folder published by the Joint Committee of Congress commemorating the Sesquicentennial was modeled on the souvenir Menu for the Centennial, a copy of which previously had been furnished by the author for that purpose.

On February 2, 1940 Charles Henry Butler became ill, and on February 9, 1940 he died.

CHAPTER XVI

PERSONALITIES OF THE UNITED STATES SUPREME COURT BENCH

MY RELATIONS WITH INDIVIDUAL MEMBERS OF THE COURT

EXCEPT IN a few sporadic instances, what has been told previously refers to my relations with the Supreme Court of the United States as a whole and not to the individual members thereof. Time and space do not, nor would the patience of my readers, permit a detailed narration of all my personal experiences with all the illustrious men who occupied seats on that high Bench from 1890, the date of my first contact with them as a member of the Judiciary Centennial Committee, to the present.

Two or three of them it had been my privilege to meet as a very young man, but during the period just mentioned it was my good fortune to become acquainted with just one less than one-half of all who have been commissioned as Chief Justices and Associate Justices of the United States. The acquaintance made prior to my Reportership—except as to those mentioned in an earlier chapter—was rather casual. But as to the twenty-nine men who have sat on the Bench since my becoming an officer of the Court, acquaintance has in many instances ripened into friendship,—and as to some into affectionate and, I hope, reciprocated regard.

So long as we occupied our Eye Street home we were fortunate in being able to entertain them as our guests, and the names of twenty-five are inscribed in our Guest Book. These names include those of Chief Justices Fuller, White, Taft and Hughes and the names of all the Associate Justices

152

commissioned after my appointment in 1902 until the house crumbled into dust to make way for an automobile parking place and gas station. In that respect, as someone facetiously remarked, the spot continued to be "a filling station."

During my Reportership we regularly attended the New Year's Day receptions in the White House. At that function the President received all Washington officialdom. Commencing at eleven o'clock in the morning, the members of the Cabinet started the line of guests; then came the members of the Diplomatic Corps to pay their respects; and after them followed the Chief Justice and the Associate Justices and officers of the Supreme Court and the rest of the Federal Judiciary and members of their families, all wishing the Chief Executive and the First Lady of the Land the compliments of the season.

After passing the line we emerged into the East Room, and those of us who had been asked to do so, went "back of the line" into the Blue Room. With those assembled there we exchanged New Year's greetings and then returned to our homes. Following luncheon the male members of the family made their New Year's calls on the Cabinet ladies, who in the early years of this century were "at home" at two o'clock in the afternoon. The diplomats, however, as well as a few favored guests, sometimes including ourselves, attended also the annual New Year's Day breakfast given by the Secretary of State at half past one.

It occurred to Mrs. Butler and myself that the two hours "Between the White House and the Calls," as described on our invitation cards, might be utilized for entertainment purposes. So the New Year's Breakfasts at 1535 Eye Street were instituted.

Chief Justice Fuller accepted our invitation to be the guest of honor at the first of these breakfasts which was given on New Year's Day 1909. About fifty guests, mostly justices

153

Mr. Justice Harlan
accepts with pleasure
the invitation of Mr.
Charles Henry Butler
to breakfast on the
3rd day of January
1910 at 12.30 o'clock
to meet the Chief
Justice of the United
States.

Dec 21st 1909

of the Supreme and other courts and members of the Bar
were asked to meet him. The experiment proved a success
and the breakfasts were continued until New Year's Day
1925 when the last one was held. After that time my wife's
health did not permit any elaborate entertainment at our
Eye Street home.

In 1915 we had a similar breakfast on Washington's Birthday, but on a larger scale. All the viands, except the coffee,
sugar and cigars, consisted of products of our summer home,

Montsweag Farm in Maine. From 1916 on we combined
the New Year's and the Farm breakfasts into what were
known as the New Year Montsweag Farm Breakfasts, which
were continued annually except during the World War. In
1918 a New Year's Eve reception to the Serbian Legation
took the place of the breakfast. It was omitted entirely in
1919 at the public request of Mr. Herbert Hoover, Food Ad-
ministrator, because all entertainment was being curtailed
at that time.

To these breakfasts the Chief Justice and other members
of the Court were always invited and most of them came
nearly every New Year's Day, as did also many members of
the Diplomatic Corps. They were very delightful occasions
and achieved quite a reputation. At first they were "stags,"
although Mrs. Butler asked a few of her lady friends to
assist her in receiving the guests. Each year more and more
ladies were added to her list and during the latter years the
breakfasts lost their strictly masculine character.

Our apple orchard at Montsweag Farm became noted and
our McIntosh Red Apples had more than a State-wide reputation. Every year, until the thirties, it was my custom
during the early part of the session to send to the Robing
Room of the Supreme Court a basket of these apples to be
eaten at luncheon by the Justices and to be distributed to the
Staff. That the contents of the basket were enjoyed is evident from letters received in regard thereto.

At the first conference held by the Court after March 5,
1932 the Justices, assembled in the Robing Room in the Capitol where they took luncheon, received a communication
from me in the form of a petition, which recited the fact that
the members of my grandfather's family had been members
of the Bar of the Court for one hundred consecutive years.
The petition prayed that the occasion would be appropriately marked by their partaking of the Montsweag Farm Mc-
Intosh Red Apples, which accompanied the petition, and ac-
cepting them as evidence that even if my grandfather's fam-

155

Supreme Court of the United States
Washington, D.C.

Christmas 1926

My Dear Butler.

You grow the most beautiful apples in the world and I thank you warmly for giving me a specimen of your wonders. I appreciate your kindness and trust you and yours a happy New Year.

[signature]

---

ily had in any way deteriorated as far as legal ability was concerned, it still maintained its ability for the production of apples. The Chief Justice assured me that the apples had been received, enjoyed, and "were duly eaten in your honor."

Dec. 25th 1927

Supreme Court of the United States
Washington, D.C.

Dear Charles Henry

Thank you for the apples. You are ever faithful. With best wishes for the New Year

Sincerely yours

Wm H Taft

Charles Henry Butler Esq

Washington 1535 I Street

After Mrs. Butler's death in 1928 Montsweag Farm was not the place it had been before. Later the depression prevented keeping it up as it had been kept. The orchard was leased, the distribution of the McIntosh Reds was discontinued; and later still the Farm was sold. Soon after the buildings were burned to the ground. All that now remains of Montsweag Farm are memories of the place and the apples and the New Year's Day Breakfasts; but those memories are ineffaceable. The Guest Book record shows the attendance at one or more of these gatherings, of Chief Justice Fuller, Chief Justice Taft, Justices Van Devanter,

157

Supreme Court of the United States
Washington, D.C.

April 17, 1932

My dear Butler

The old days when
I had the privilege of
sending messages from
Albany to your dear mother—
and your hospitality in
the early visits to Washington
stand out very clearly in
my memory, and your
good word is the more
appreciated because of

[handwritten note]

our old friendship · By the
way, the apples were
duly eaten in your honor. —
Faithfully yours,

Charles E. Hughes

Hon. Charles Henry Butler

Holmes, McReynolds, Stone and other members of the
Supreme Court Bench.

In relating my recollections of various Justices it is not my
intention to make a chronological recital of personal anecdotes covering the first half of the second century of the
Court's existence, but to recall some of the pleasant episodes
involving members of the Court and myself.

Justice Samuel Nelson, who served from 1845 to 1872,
lived after his retirement at his home in Cooperstown, New
York, where our family spent a summer during my youth.
Thus there was afforded me the pleasure of meeting this
very able jurist and picturesque old gentleman, who had
presided at the memorial meeting held for my grandfather
in 1859. In Washington, more than fifty years later, it was
my pleasure to meet his grand-daughter, Mrs. Loesch, wife
of that famous crime enemy, Judge Frank J. Loesch of Chicago. She told me of the search being made for her grandfather's portrait which had been mislaid. It was finally

Feb. 25, 1932

Dear Mr. Butler,

I am happy that you are happy — and that the apples are red and ripe.

Many, many thanks

Faithfully yours,

Benjamin N. Cardozo

Mr. Chas. Henry Butler

---

traced by the Marshal of the Court and now hangs in the Counsel Conference Room of the Supreme Court Building.

Chief Justice Morrison R. Waite, who served from 1874 to 1888, while the Court still went on Circuit, held Circuit Courts in New York. As my duties were in the Admiralty branch of my father's office, it was not infrequently that I was in Justice Waite's Court Room as an assistant to the partner of the firm pleading before him.

Before going on the Bench (1882-1893) Justice Samuel A.

160

HENRY F. BUTLER

THOMAS ENNALS WAGGAMAN

Marshal of the Supreme Court

CHARLES ELMORE CROPLEY

Clerk of the Supreme Court

Blatchford practiced law in New York. He was always a friend of my father. When promoted to become Justice Blatchford, from his position as Judge of the United States District Court, my father was asked to take that post. He declined the offer, however, for, as he himself put it, he was under the necessity of feeding and providing with shoes his wife and eight children.

Justice Noah H. Swayne, who served from 1862 to 1881, came to New York after his retirement and was a great friend of my uncle, Charles Butler, at whose home we met him often. In my class at Princeton was a son of Justice William Strong (1870-1880) with whom we came in contact on several occasions.

The foregoing is the basis of the statement that probably few, if anyone except myself, have known an appointee of President Tyler who took his seat in 1845, [Justice Samuel Nelson]; all the Chief Justices since Salmon P. Chase; and all the Justices appointed since the time of President Buchanan excepting four. One of the four, Mr. Stanton, never sat on the Bench. His son also was a Princeton classmate of mine.

Nearly one-third of all these Chief Justices and Justices it has been my honor and pleasure to entertain in my home; and my family have in their possession personal letters from more than one-half of all who have graced that illustrious Bench.

CHIEF JUSTICE MELVILLE WESTON FULLER (1888-1910)

FORGETTING HIM for a moment as the highest judicial officer of the country, Chief Justice Melville Weston Fuller was a most lovable character. He was full of humanity, had a great deal of humor, and was a devout Christian. All this was referred to at more length in the chapter entitled "Memorial Tributes." In his youth he must have been a rather jolly boon companion as evidenced by the following Bacchanalian Song written by him for one of the reunions of his Class of '53 at his Alma Mater, Bowdoin College, Brunswick, Maine.

BACCHANALIAN SONG *

BY MELVILLE WESTON FULLER

Gaily the wine in our goblets is gleaming,
Bright on its surface the foam bubbles swim,
So the smiles of our joy from each countenance beaming
Are the bubbles that dance on the cup of life's brim.

Oh, what are life's hopes and its high aspirations,
But wishes for things that are not what they seem?
Away to the shades with such dull contemplations,
Utopian visions where all is a dream,—

The flag at our masthead is pleasure's own banner,
And to the breeze boldly its broad folds we fling,
While each stout-hearted sailor will raise the hosanna
To ivy-crowned Bacchus, our jolly-souled King.

Then fill up your glasses, lads, fill up your glasses,
With frolicksome pleasure the moments employ,
Since life is a span, each bright hour it passes,
When seized on its flight it is ours to enjoy.

Although Chief Justice Fuller's patience was often strained in the Court Room, he was never heard to speak except in the kindliest manner to counsel; and it was not unusual to hear him gently assist an attorney addressing the Court for the first time.

Frequently it was his lot, as befalls all presiding justices, to have to remind counsel that the allotted time had expired; and he always did so with firmness, but generally with a smile. On one occasion the Attorney General of Hawaii, appearing for the first time in the Supreme Court, commenced his argument in the afternoon and proceeded in a very leisurely manner to discuss in general terms the advan-

* From "The Native Poets of Maine"—David Bugbee & Co., Bangor, Maine, 1854, p. 298. (Also printed in The Gift Book of Gems, David Bugbee & Co., Bangor, 1886.)

tages of the annexation of his country to the United States, with very slight reference to the main points involved in the case he was arguing. The following morning, as the Attorney General of Hawaii rose to resume his argument, he informed the Court that he had not been aware of the then two-hour rule and was greatly disturbed.

Chief Justice Fuller called his attention to the fact that he had already used up three-quarters of an hour and asked how much time he needed.

"Why, Your Honor," said the Attorney General of Hawaii, "I have barely just begun."

"This is really most distressing," observed the Chief Justice.

Thereupon the Hawaiian Attorney General announced that Solicitor General Hoyt had told him he could have some of the Solicitor General's time. Solicitor General Hoyt immediately stood up to explain that he had only said that he did not expect to use all his own time. The Chief Justice interposed:

"Mr. Solicitor General, I understand your position; but, Mr. Attorney General, the time not used by counsel does not belong to him to dispose of. It reverts to the Court." Then with his very charming smile the Chief Justice added: "Now, Mr. Attorney General, we will forget that you used any of your time yesterday and will begin all over again this morning."

Then the Chief Justice suggested that the opening statement convey some idea as to the facts and the law in the case, rather than the general advantages of annexation.

The role of the Chief Justice is not in all respects an easy one. He has to do many things which the public, or even members of the Bar, never know. Chief Justice Fuller told me once that an Associate Justice, who had delivered the majority opinion reversing the Court below, informed him that the dissenting Justice had obtained my promise to include as a footnote the entire opinion of the lower Court.

163

Sunday Evening

Dear Mr. Butler,

We have just gotten back from our farm, where we spent Christmas. On our arrival we found the box of apples you were good enough to send. I'm sorry to have to confess that we can produce nothing like them. I am eating one as I write this, and I never tasted a

---

This was a great surprise to me because no such promise had been made, nor would any such footnote be made in that or any other case. My assurance to the Chief Justice to that effect greatly relieved him. During this interview he rather unburdened his soul to me as to the various difficulties Chief Justices experience besides those of writing opinions.

The Chief Justice gave a dinner to Mr. Justice Day, to

better.

Mrs Roberts asks me to thank you on her behalf.

Happy New Year to you

Yours Sincerely

Oliver J Roberts;

Charles Henry Butler, Esqr;

---

which he invited me; and it was a most enjoyable affair. While coffee was being served in the drawing-room, a young officer called to say good-by to the Chief Justice and Mrs. Fuller. He had been suddenly ordered to the Philippines and was leaving Washington the next day. After having received the dinner guests, Mrs. Fuller had retired upstairs; yet while the Chief Justice was making excuses for her, she called from the floor above to the young officer, and said that though she could not come downstairs, she would talk to him over the bannisters.

After the exchange of farewells, and just as the young officer was going out the front door, Mrs. Fuller called to him by his first name and said:

"And when you get to the Philippines, you tell Willie Taft not to be in too much of a hurry to get into my husband's shoes."

The Chief Justice and his guests greeted this final message with a hearty laugh.

After having been Solicitor General of the United States and Circuit Judge for the Sixth Circuit, Mr. Taft was then High Commissioner to the Philippines. Eventually he became Chief Justice, yet he did not step into the shoes of Chief Justice Fuller, but into those of his own appointee when he was President, Chief Justice Edward D. White.

Chief Justice Fuller was always assigned to the Third Circuit and occasionally held Court in Richmond, Virginia, where frequently he was the guest of a friend living in one of the old Colonial suburban mansions. On one visit, when the weather was very warm, Sam, the colored majordomo of the house is reported to have said:

"Mr. Chief Justice, when you was here before I made you a mint julep, which you 'lowed went to der right spot. Would you like me to make you anoder one now?"

"Yes, indeed, Sam."

After the julep had been duly served and enjoyed, as Sam was removing the empty glass, he inquired:

"Mr. Chief Justice, did dat julep go to der right spot?"

"Yes, Sam, it did go to the right spot," and as Sam was moving away smiling, the Chief Justice added: "But, Sam, there are *two* spots."

This story is told as cumulative evidence of the charming and human characteristics of the man who could function as the highest judicial officer of the country, and at the same time enjoy life and give pleasure to those around him.

CHIEF JUSTICE CHARLES EVANS HUGHES (1930-   *)

PRIOR TO 1910 a very pleasant friendship existed between the Butler family and that of Charles Evans Hughes and so his appointment as Associate Justice of the Supreme Court by President Taft, to fill the vacancy caused by the death

* Chief Justice Hughes retired in 1941. Ed.

of Justice Brewer, was most gratifying to us. As New Yorkers, however, we were sorry to lose such a good Governor of the State as he had proved himself to be.

Because his appointment and confirmation did not occur until after the Court had adjourned for the term, Governor Hughes remained at Albany and performed his duties as Governor until the Court reconvened on October 10, 1910. He then ascended the Bench where he remained until June 1916, when he resigned to accept the presidential nomination of the Republican Party.

After his confirmation and during the Court's vacation, visits were exchanged between the Executive Mansion in Albany, where Mrs. Butler and I stopped while motoring from Washington to Montsweag Farm in Maine, and our Eye Street home where the Governor and Mrs. Hughes came in order to choose their residence in the nation's capital. On the first occasion the Governor was accompanied only by his aides and, as Mrs. Butler was in Maine, we kept bachelors' hall.

At one of our dinners were Assistant Secretary of State and the then Mrs. Huntington Wilson, since deceased, who was a brilliant conversationalist. In Mrs. Butler's absence she had been asked to act as hostess, and the Governor sat at her right. The talk was general, and at one stage the Governor said:

"Butler, what was the 'color line of the Court' I heard someone refer to the other day?"

"That," was my reply, "was when Justices Gray, Brown, and White sat in a row; but as only Justice White is left there is no color in the Court now."

"Oh, no, Mr. Butler," said Mrs. Wilson, quick as a flash, "the Court is all Hughes now."

This *mot* was happily received by all and the dinner was a great success. Before leaving the Governor made a record of his visit in the Guest Book, alluding to a newspaper article about his house-hunting activities, both of which are here reproduced.

167

Governor Hughes is still on the hunt for a house.

Yet it is far from a "still hunt." He spent the entire day yesterday examining, with Mrs. Hughes, various pieces of Washington property, but they were unable to reach a conclusion as to the most desirable.

Today the distinguished New Yorker again fared forth to look at some new offerings. Various agents advised him of holdings which they believed would just suit and as none of the houses already seen exactly suited, the governor decided to see all that were available before finally deciding which to buy.

When he left Washington after his first trip he had made up his mind to rent a place for a year. In the meantime he expected to cast about for a house that would meet his needs. Since returning here, however, he has decided to purchase a place now and avoid moving twice.

It was said at the Butler home this morning that the governor, Mrs. Hughes and Major Crossett, his secretary, probably will leave for Albany tomorrow morning.

With appreciation of your hospitality, diplomacy and protecting care during this "open season" —

July 15ᵗʰ 1910 (July & Aug?)   Charles E. Hughes

Jr.? Antoinette C. Hughes.

July 15. 1910 (& Aug?)   Frederick M. Crossett

On another visit to Washington Mrs. Hughes accompanied the Governor; and the impressions left of the visits of the then Governor-Justice and now Chief Justice have always been among the pleasantest memories still lingering over the period of the Eye Street occupancy.

Justice John Marshall Harlan (1877-1911)

Justice Harlan was one of the "great dissenters" of the Court. He was very emphatic in his utterances and more than once began his oral statement with an expression to the effect that the wise framers of our Constitution would turn in their graves if they knew how this Court, which they had established to preserve the integrity of the Constitution was misconstruing that instrument in a manner that must ultimately destroy the fundamental rights and liberty of the nation.

Such were his sentiments, however they may have been expressed, in connection with the five to four decision in the Standard Oil anti-trust case. Justice White delivered the opinion of the Court and for the first time in that series of cases, resorted to the "rule of reason" theory. Justice Harlan's written dissent, strong as it was, was not so positive as the one he uttered orally in much more vigorous terms from the Bench.

The next morning, while Justice McKenna and myself were in a trolley on our way to the Capitol, Senator Knox—formerly United States Attorney General—entered the car. He seated himself opposite us and after good-morning greetings had been exchanged, Justice McKenna asked:

"What do you think of the Court now?"

"Well," Senator Knox responded, "I should hate to use any such language about the Court as it said about itself yesterday."

That was in 1911; and not until Mr. Justice McReynolds delivered his opinion in the Gold Clause Cases was it ever my lot to hear such a vigorous dissent again.

169

On Justice Harlan's seventieth birthday, June 1, 1903, we gave him a reception at our Eye Street home. For two weeks it had been unprecedentedly hot. In those days we dressed less sensibly than we do now; men appeared at many afternoon and evening functions in summer in the same attire they wore during the winter season. Accordingly and at my request there appeared in the social columns of the evening newspapers that afternoon a paragraph to the effect that Mr. Butler hoped his guests at the Harlan reception would come in comfortable dress and that he would receive them in a white dinner suit. When the newspapers came out the thermometer was in the nineties.

Before nine o'clock the mercury had dropped to about fifty and our guests were coming in overcoats. The promise of the host to appear in summer attire was, however, fulfilled. Such changes as this in the temperature probably prompted the beloved late Will Rogers to advise caution in criticizing or extolling Washington weather, when he said that whatever it might be at the time of our remarks, it would probably be entirely different one or two hours later.

In 1905 a case * was decided by the United States Supreme Court which is generally referred to as the New York Bakers' Case. It involved the constitutionality of certain provisions in the New York Labor Law relating to and regulating the Bakers' trade. The law contained a provision limiting the hours of labor in biscuit, bread, cake and confectionery establishments to not more than sixty hours a week.

The unpublished background of the case is that one of the attorneys, who was a young journeyman baker when the Act was passed, was convinced of its unconstitutionality—under the Fourteenth Amendment—as interfering with the right of contract between employers and employees. Determined to have it so declared by the Courts, he studied law and was admitted to the Bar of New York State. He arranged to

* (Lochner v. New York 198 U.S. 45.)

170

appear in a case in the Criminal Court in which an employer was convicted of violating the labor provision of the law and was fined $50.00.

Unsuccessful appeals were taken to the Appellate Division and to the Court of Appeals. Under the then existing practice the case was brought up on error to the Supreme Court of the United States where the law was declared unconstitutional. The young attorney, who had at first been a baker, had not been a member of the New York Bar for three years and so was not eligible for admission to the Supreme Court Bar. Yet he was specially admitted *pro hac vice* for the purpose of arguing this case. On his first appearance before the Court he won a signal victory, although by the narrow margin of a five to four decision.

There was one rather amusing element in the record of this case. Some sections of the Act provided regulations of one sort or another for "any biscuit, bread, *pie*, or cake bakery;" but the hours of labor section related only to a "biscuit, bread, or cake bakery." The word *pie* was omitted.

One of the contentions in regard to unequal protection of the law was that, as there was no proper basis for limiting the hours of labor in "biscuit, bread, and cake bakeries," and not doing the same in regard to "pie bakeries" an unequal burden was placed on all other bakeries. To show that this was not such a fatal inequality evidence was produced to the effect that there was a sufficiently reasonable difference between pie bakeries and other bakeries to justify this incongruity.

As a matter of fact, however, the engrosser, while copying the Act for the Governor's signature, accidentally omitted the word "pie" from Section 110. Thus whatever might have been the intention of the Legislature, the Act as signed controlled the situation. The decision turned on a broader point, however, and so this element was not referred to in the opinion.

Yet it was entertaining to read the testimony taken in

regard to this phase of the case while knowing that everybody on the Bench, at the Bar, and in the audience was aware that the Legislature never had any intention of relieving pie bakeries from the burden of the hours and the labor provision which an error of penmanship had given them.

The decision of the Court was a surprise to many, including myself, and when the opinions reached me, to be edited and published in Volume 198 of the Official Reports, it seemed to me that the opinions had shifted, and that the dissent of Justice Harlan must originally have been written as the opinion of the Court and that of Justice Peckham as a dissent.

This notion was confirmed years later. After Justice Harlan's death my brother-in-law, John Maynard Harlan, told me that his father had confided to him that the case had originally been assigned to him for the opinion of the Court, but that at a subsequent conference it had been transferred to Justice Peckham, which resulted in Justice Harlan changing his own opinion to a dissent. It was not divulged which one of the Justices had shifted his position. In my humble judgment Justice Harlan's dissent in this case would today be regarded as expressing the opinion of the Court in regard to the subject matter involved rather than the majority opinion of Justice Peckham.

Justice Harlan's grandson, John Marshall Harlan II, a member of the New York law firm founded by Elihu Root, is my nephew by marriage. The Justice's son John Maynard Harlan, married Mrs. Butler's younger sister, and so the Harlan and Butler families were relatives as well as friends. His oldest son Richard D. was a member of my class at Princeton.

Justice Harlan was Senior Justice for more than two-thirds of the period of my Reportership, and my appointment was largely due to his influence. He was appointed to the Court by President Hayes in 1877, nearly eleven years before Chief

Justice Fuller was appointed, and occupied the seat on his right after the resignation of Justice Field.

He died in 1911 after serving nearly thirty-four years; but he did not realize either his hope of having had the longest tenure of office, or his other hope of becoming Chief Justice after the death of Chief Justice Fuller. Mr. Justice Field and Chief Justice Marshall both served somewhat more than thirty-four years.

When Chief Justice Fuller died there was of course much speculation as to his successor. If a member of the Court was to be promoted to "sit under the clock," as the post of Chief Justice is frequently referred to, it seemed only natural that it would be Mr. Justice Harlan. During his term of service of more than one-third of a century he had gradually worked his way from the chair on the extreme left to that on the right of the Chief Justice; and after the death of Chief Justice Fuller had acted temporarily in that capacity. Very naturally Justice Harlan may have had the same thought.

Suddenly came the announcement that President Taft, who was a Republican and a Protestant, had passed over the Senior Justice of his own party and faith, and had nominated Mr. Justice White, a Democrat and a Roman Catholic, to be Chief Justice of the United States. The nomination was soon confirmed.

One of the events always to be remembered by those who witnessed it, was the administration of the oath of office to Chief Justice White by Justice Harlan at the first session of the Court after such confirmation. On that occasion Justice Harlan, who was sitting temporarily in the Chief Justice's chair, announced the appointment and confirmation of Chief Justice Fuller's successor and administered the oath to his colleague who, as Senior Justice next in order, was sitting in the seat theretofore occupied by Justice Harlan. When the oath had been administered and Justice White had actually become Chief Justice, the two Justices ex-

...., 190

I have been sending to you for 2 weeks some dry wine — a pig full — but my man has neglected my orders. It will go to you to-night or to morrow or some-body will be —

I will not forget to-morrow night H

Notes from Justice Harlan to the Author

Monday

Dear Butler

Of course

I will come.

John Marshall Harlan

changed places and the business of the Court proceeded.

Although there can be no doubt that Justice Harlan was deeply disappointed, he never once betrayed any feeling on the subject and continued with unabated strength his work on the Court. He died less than a year thereafter.

JUSTICE OLIVER WENDELL HOLMES (1902-1932)

WHEN Associate Justice Horace Gray was appointed by President Hayes in 1881, he was Chief Justice of the Supreme Judicial Court of Massachusetts. He died in 1902 during the vacation of the Court. President Theodore Roosevelt appointed as his successor Oliver Wendell Holmes who at the time also was Chief Justice of the Supreme Judicial Court of Massachusetts.

On Monday, December 8, 1902 Mr. Justice Holmes took the oath and was escorted by the Clerk to the seat on the extreme left of the Bench where the most recently named Justice always sits. Deaths and resignations of his seniors occurred, however and when Justice McKenna resigned in 1925 Justice Holmes became Senior Justice and sat thereafter at the right of the Chief Justice until his resignation in 1932.

We were intimately and pleasantly acquainted with Justice and Mrs. Holmes. They were frequently at our home as we were at theirs. They purchased and lived at No. 1720 Eye Street, N. W., about two blocks west of our house. The property forms a part of the residuary estate, which by the Justice's last will and testament, was bequeathed to the United States of America.

Our arrivals in Washington having been practically simultaneous, we were both on the outlook for residential property at the same time. No. 1720 Eye Street had been offered to us, and we were seriously considering buying it. Hearing, however, that Justice Holmes also was considering the house, we withdrew from what, had the bidder been anyone else, might have been a contest for possession. In nearly all real estate negotiations, "there is another party who wants the property." This alleged desire of acquisition is used by the broker to bring the sale to a conclusion. That "other party" generally is as mythical as the ogre invented by nurses to frighten children who are recalcitrant about going to bed.

For once, however, it happened that the prospects were real and not visionary. Our withdrawal from the field left it open to Justice and Mrs. Holmes to acquire the property, which they did and lived there happily ever afterwards. Very soon we bought 1535 Eye Street where we also lived very happily until Mrs. Butler's death in 1928. A few years later the property was disposed of.

The Justice constantly attended our New Year's and Montsweag Farm Breakfasts as long as they continued; and he and Mrs. Holmes frequently accepted other invitations to entertainments at our Eye Street residence. He was a most delightful guest, as he thoroughly understood and practised the art of conversation, which, he himself said, seemed to be dying out in America. This was evidenced, he held, by the introduction of various methods of entertainment at dinners which were wholly unknown in what he called the "Golden Days of American Entertainment."

Justice Holmes was not only a very handsome man, but also exceedingly gallant in his conduct toward and conversation with the ladies. Naturally he and Mrs. Holmes, who was charming both as guest and hostess, were much sought after. His birthday was on the eighth of March and, on one occasion, in answering an invitation of Mrs. Butler, which he had to decline, he concluded: "Your venerable friend," and added at the bottom of the page: "P.S. I am 65 today."

No one ever regarded him as "venerable" at that age because he was exceedingly spry and active; and for more than a quarter of a century thereafter he still occupied his seat on the Bench.

On his seventy-fifth birthday as we passed Shaffer's floral

THE PRESENT SUPREME COURT BUILDING

ERNEST KNAEBEL

Reporter of the Decisions of the Supreme Court
of the United States

THE PRESENT SUPREME COURT ROOM

Supreme Court of the United States,
Washington, D.C.

March 8/06

Dear Mr. Butler

I fear that I shall not be able to accept your kind invitation for tomorrow — I thank you none the less for the thought.

Your venerable friend

O.W. Holmes

(I am 65 today)

---

establishment, about a block away from our Eye Street home, Mrs. Butler requested me to purchase *one* of a display of magnificent American Beauty roses in the window. Acceding to her request, but asking why just one rose, she replied:

"You will see when we get home."

On arriving there, she wrote on her card: "An American Beauty for an American beauty."

She put the card in an envelope and directed the chauffeur to deliver it and the rose to Justice Holmes. Later during the day there came an acknowledgment from Justice Holmes in which he wrote that the word "for" should have been "from."

Thus started our custom of sending on every succeeding birthday a single red rose to the Justice. It always came from Mrs. Butler until her death; after that it was sent by me and generally delivered in person, but always in her memory. This was so on his last birthday in 1931. The next day, one of the newspapers called attention to the fact that, among those paying their birthday respects to the Justice, "came Charles Henry Butler bearing, as usual, a single red rose." When the Justice passed away, my final tribute was the same, handed to one of his nieces who, greeting me at the door, said she had hoped my tribute would be just such a rose, as her uncle had often told her of our custom.

One afternoon the Justice and I met at the Capitol and his suggestion that we walk home together was most agreeable to me. Half way down Capitol Hill he suddenly grabbed my arm and said:

"That's a fire engine, isn't it?"

On my replying that it was, he exclaimed: "I always go to fires, don't you?"

To my affirmative response he returned: "Let's go."

We located that fire as being a nearby lumber mill on Maryland Avenue and changed our course accordingly. Then the Justice said:

"In Boston we always *run* to fires. Don't you think we'd better *run?*"

Again I replied in the affirmative, and we both started at a dog-trot down Capitol Hill and up Maryland Avenue where we witnessed what he described as "an awfully jolly good fire." It certainly was. We watched the flames until we suddenly realized that it was time for us to get back to our respective homes and prepare for the evening entertainments to which we had both been committed by the respective rulers of our households. He told me that whenever there was a fire in any direction he would be glad to go to it with me even if he had to be routed out of bed. In fact it would not have surprised me had he left the Bench to witness a fire while the Court was in session. He also told me that Mrs. Holmes was equally fond of such spectacles.

While Halley's Comet was cavorting around and making an exhibition of itself in the evenings during the summer of 1910, the Justice and Mrs. Holmes participated in a visit to the Naval Observatory on Massachusetts Avenue. We all enjoyed ourselves very much under the guidance and instruction of Commodore Veedra, then Superintendent of the Observatory. During the evening Justice Holmes and Mrs. Holmes became separated, each joining a party going in a different direction from the other; and the mix-up did not get straightened out until nearly two o'clock in the morning. When the Justice turned up in Court the next day, he told me he had never before in his life had such a good time.

On more than one occasion Mrs. Butler and I stopped at the Beverly Farms home of Justice Holmes while on our way to and from Montsweag Farm. Once we spent a weekend with them which was a most delightful and long remembered episode.

Justice Holmes was very meticulous—a word he frequently used himself—about the printing and publishing of his opinions. He examined the proof sheets of his opinions carefully before they were distributed by the Clerk.

On my desk one morning was a page of the current advance sheets of the Reports with a correction marked, and a rather tart note from the Justice about the inexcusability of an error he had discovered. Just as my reply memorandum was being completed, in which it was explained to the Justice that the error had already been detected by myself, and a correction sent to the printer, the Clerk handed me a printed copy of the latest opinion of the Justice, who always personally corrected the Clerk's copies. The same overlooking Providence that has been credited with taking care of sailors, drunken men, babies, and the United States, came to my rescue this time by including Reporters of the Decisions of the Supreme Court of the United States.

Fortunately for me the Justice had made a serious and plainly evident error of grammar in one of the sentences in this latest opinion. Marking the error I added a postscript:

"Has your Honor any suggestions to make as to the annexed?"

In a few minutes back came a reply from him in which he admitted that my shot had got him very prettily.

More than once Justice Holmes told me personally about his views, so often expressed in his opinions, that no legislative action, State or Federal, was unconstitutional unless so clearly violative of express written provisions of the controlling Constitution that there could be absolutely no doubt as to the lack of power to enact it.

He believed in the parliamentary power of the legislature except where such limitations positively prohibited action of the enacting body. Consequently he was often on the dissenting side of the Court when the majority declared State or Federal legislative action inoperative as being unconstitutional. By the same token his opinions were often unacceptable to the ultra, and even to the more moderate conservative elements of society.

On a certain afternoon at the Metropolitan Club, while I was speaking to a group of members in the lobby and claiming to have rendered a service to the country by safely escorting Justice Holmes, then well in his eighties, across

Supreme Court of the United States,
Washington, D.C.

Jan 16/ 1911

Dear dear Reporter

I thought that
you would see that I cut it into
a thick — but you have got back
on her old rights — The Error in
the print but to me is plain and
— Correct it,

Yours very truly

[signature]

---

several street crossings as he was returning alone to his
home, one member exclaimed:

"Butler, you think you have rendered the Country a service by saving the life of Justice Holmes. I don't. I think
you ought to be indicted."

Evidently this member was one of those who disagreed
with the Justice's ideas in regard to regulatory legislative
power.

A former colleague of Justice Holmes on the Bench, who

181

was of much more conservative tendencies, to whom this story was told, said that he could well appreciate the situation and the feelings of the man who thought that the automotive death toll should not have been interfered with by keeping the name of Justice Holmes off its list.

When State Police Legislation was held by the Court to be unconstitutional, Justice Holmes frequently dissented from the majority, either writing the dissenting opinion himself, or concurring in one written by Justice Brandeis or by Justice Clarke.

These three generally stood together in that respect as closely as Dumas' "Three Musketeers." On one occasion after Justice Holmes had orally delivered a dissent, he added:

"I am authorized to say that Mr. Justice Brandeis concurs in this dissent."

Listeners within the Bar looked in surprise at each other as the next Justice began to deliver an opinion. But as soon as he had finished the mystery was cleared up when Justice Holmes said:

"I should have said in delivering my last dissent that Mr. Justice Clarke, as well as Mr. Justice Brandeis, concurs."

There was a perceptible feeling of relief as none of the listeners familiar with the individual tendencies of the Justices understood just what rift might have occurred between the three inseparables.

A secretary of Justice Holmes told me that once when he arrived at the Justice's office rather late he made excuse for his tardiness; and also explained to Justice Holmes that his breath might indicate he had not come directly from the breakfast table. In fact the secretary admitted, he had stopped on his way to the Justice's office, as some friends were leaving Washington that morning and there had been a little celebration. On hearing this Justice Holmes observed:

"Yes, I can visualize a rather long mahogany counter, on

which one's arm can rest while holding a goblet with something in it, and below is a brass rail on which one foot is
resting. Thinking of this makes me regret some of the limitations imposed on one who occupies my position."

The Justice's secretary proceeded with his duties, greatly
relieved by the Justice's reception of the reason given for his
lateness.

Much has been written about Justice Holmes, especially in
regard to his legal attainments, his philosophy and his place
in law and literature. The few incidents related here are
told simply to show that there was a great deal to him
besides legal ability. He was exceedingly human. He had
many and delightful social tendencies. He was full of
humor and a most charming companion. I have nearly one
hundred letters and other written communications from
him which I prize, and these personal recollections of him
are among my most valued possessions.

Justice Moody (1906-1910)

WILLIAM H. MOODY was a member of Congress from the
Newburyport and Gloucester District of Massachusetts. He
was a Harvard man and a friend of President Roosevelt,
who appointed him first to be Secretary of the Navy and
then Attorney General. He used to ride horseback nearly
every afternoon and chose the same area for his equestrian
exercise as mine, Potomac Park. General William Crozier
and Congressman, afterwards Senator, Gillette and Secretary Moody, at that time all bachelors, were great friends,
and lived together in bachelor quarters. This ménage was
broken up later. Crozier married Mrs. May Williams, and
Gillette married the widow of Congressman Rockwood
Hoar, thus leaving Moody alone in his bachelor quarters.

We met many afternoons while exercising our respective
steeds and became very close friends. As Attorney General

he used to appear quite frequently in the Supreme Court Room, although my memory recalls only one case in which he actually made the argument. After the retirement of Justice Brown, President Theodore Roosevelt asked Secretary of War Taft to accept nomination to the Bench and there was immediate speculation as to whether Mr. Taft would accept it. One day Moody said to me:

"Butler, you may see me up on the Hill before long."

When I replied it would be a pleasure to welcome him, but expressed some surprise that the vacant seat was not to be filled by his Cabinet colleague, Moody informed me:

"When Taft arrived this morning at the Cabinet meeting the President said: 'Here comes the man who has spoiled all my plans for strengthening the Supreme Court. Now, Will, what do you mean by doing that?' 'Well,' answered Secretary Taft, 'what can a man do except surrender when all the females in the family get around and fight him with a battery of tears?'

"And so," Moody added, "the President says he can't do anything else but appoint me."

Sure enough a few days later his nomination was presented to the Senate. It was confirmed and he took his seat in December, 1906 and served until 1910.

There is a story that while Secretary Taft was considering whether he would accept the nomination to the Bench one of his sons was asked whether his father was going to be a Supreme Court Justice. The boy answered:

"Nope."

To the further inquiry, "Why not?" the boy answered:

"Ma wants him to wait and be President."

The truth of this story is not vouched for, but if true, the youngster was a pretty good prophet.

The incident, however, may have been a paraphrase of this story which the author told Dr. Joseph Sizoo, the talented and popular rector of the New York Avenue Presbyterian Church, who had refused a call to a New York City church, but was expecting the receipt of another similar call.

"Doctor, you'll go to New York sooner or later. It will be the same in your case as in that of the country minister who had a call to the city. When one of the deacons asked the minister's little boy whether his father was going to remain with the church, the son answered in the negative. 'But,' said the deacon, 'we asked him to stay and he said he would carefully and prayerfully consider it.' 'Oh, that's all right,' the boy returned, 'Dad's in his study wrassling in prayer, but Ma's upstairs packing the trunks and we're goin' to New York.'"

Later Dr. Sizoo did accept the second call and is now one of the prominent ministers in New York City as Pastor of the Collegiate Church of St. Nicholas, Dutch Reformed Church, on Fifth Avenue.

A day or so after Justice Moody had been sworn in we were riding in the park, and he told me that after the ceremony of his induction and during the recess, several friends, including some of the fair sex, were lunching with him. One of them said:

"William, you said your appointment was for life."

"Well so it is," responded Justice Moody.

"No, it is not," said his friend. "The Clerk read your commission and I distinctly heard him say that it lasted only during your good behavior, and from my personal knowledge you won't hold that office very long."

She was right so far as his not holding the office for long, nor did he hold it for life. In fact Justice Moody was one of the few Justices who never moved from the seat he first occupied on the extreme left of the Bench, where the latest appointee always sits. The close of his life was really a tragedy.

During the early part of May, 1908 he showed signs of failing strength and was advised to take a long rest. He decided to go to Hot Springs, Virginia, for the approaching two weeks vacation of the Court and wanted me to accompany him. We reserved the drawing room on the train for our joint use; but some unfortunate combination of circumstances prevented me from making the trip—to his disappointment as well as my own. He at first thought that he also would abandon the journey planned, but later determined to go by himself. We had our last horseback ride together the afternoon of the day on which he left Washington for Hot Springs. He intended to be back when the Court reconvened, but he never sat on the Bench again. He wrote the opinions which had been assigned to him before he went to Hot Springs; and on the last opinion day of the term they were read for him by the Chief Justice. He remained for several weeks at Hot Springs after the Court had adjourned, and then went direct to his home at Haverhill, Massachusetts.

On motor trips of Mrs. Butler and myself from Washington to Montsweag Farm, we often stopped at his Haverhill home for a visit. If we were southward bound we always left some products of Montsweag Farm at Haverhill.

When it became evident that he could never resume his duties on the Bench, Congress passed an Act * permitting him to avail of the privilege of retirement under Section 714 of the Revised Statutes, notwithstanding he had not been on the Bench for ten years, or that he was not seventy years old. Justice Moody retired in 1910 and President Taft appointed Charles Evans Hughes to succeed him. Upon his retirement Justice Moody came to Washington for one winter, but after that returned to Haverhill where he remained until his death in 1917.

My partner, John A. Kratz, who had been Mr. Moody's secretary while he was Attorney General, and for whom the Justice had a deep and reciprocated affection, used to visit him as often as he could. When either of us went to see

* (Act of June 23, 1910. c. 377.)

him in Washington or at Haverhill, he would talk about the work of the Court, and tell us how he constantly kept up with the opinions, and made a note on each one, as it was rendered, of his own concurrence or dissent. It was largely through Justice Moody's interest in us both that the law firm of Butler and Kratz—which existed from immediately after my withdrawal from the Reportership until 1934—was established.

Among the many stories that Justice Moody told us while riding around Potomac Park was the following: Shortly after he became Secretary of the Navy, he visited one of the battleships with the ranking Rear Admiral of the Atlantic Fleet. As Secretary of the Navy Mr. Moody, of course, ranked above everyone on board.

After taking the necessary observations and making the calculations, according to custom at noon, the Quartermaster appeared on the quarterdeck, where the Secretary of the Navy, the Admiral of the Fleet and the Admiral in command of the battleship were standing. The Quartermaster wished to make his report. The rule is that the Quartermaster salute the commanding officer and report that it is "Eight Bells," which is the nautical term for high noon.

Thereupon the Quartermaster is told to "make it so," which means that all time-pieces on the ship are reset accordingly. However, "making it so" is the prerogative of the ranking officer. So in this case at the Quartermaster's salute, the Admiral in command of the vessel instructed him to report to the Admiral of the Fleet who in turn told the Quartermaster to report to the Secretary of the Navy. The Quartermaster obeyed instructions, and was astonished to hear from that august personage—who until then had not heard about this detail of navigation—the reply, "Thank you very much," instead of the usual "make it so."

The Admiral in command, however, whispered those necessary words to the Quartermaster, who had hardly been able to control his risibilities, and went on his way, not only to reset the clocks, but also to tell the story.

The Secretary conceded the joke was on him, and constantly during this naval visit he was in some way or other reminded of it. He had that kind of a sense of humor—alas, too rare—that can appreciate a joke even when it is on one's self.

JUSTICE DAVID J. BREWER (1889-1910)

JUSTICE BREWER, who served from 1889 until 1910, was a very lovable character, and had a quiet, but often very humorous manner of expressing himself. One evening, while I was walking home with him after a dinner we had attended, he said in reply to my inquiry as to how he had enjoyed the regular Saturday conference of the Court:

"It lasted a long time, and, Butler, you don't know how tiresome it is to have to discuss legal problems with eight other men, none of whom knows any law."

My return comment was that one or more dissents could be expected when the Court delivered its opinions on Monday, and it turned out to be correct.

Justice Brewer was a recognized authority on International Law, and in 1906 we collaborated in preparing an article on that subject contained in the "Cyclopaedia of Law and Procedure," published by the American Law Book Company, and known as "Cyc." In looking over the article while writing this book, a particular sentence caught my eye under the head "Acquisition of Territory," namely:

"Conquest:—the right of the victorious nation to retain the ownership of invaded and conquered territory is still recognized by international law. Note 88."

The authorities in Note 88 sustaining this proposition are sections in Oppenheim, and in Butler's "Treaty-Making Power of the United States," my own work on that subject which was published in 1902. My native modesty made me wonder why it had been necessary to cite Oppenheim—just as when some one told Whistler he was the best painter since Velasquez, Whistler remarked:

"Why drag that fellow in?"

It is doubtful whether Mussolini has ever seen this statement by Justice Brewer and my brief treatise on International Law, but if he has he may be relying on it to retain Ethiopia.

Justice Brewer was also exceedingly well versed in regard to the relations of the United States and the Indian Tribes. He wrote the opinions of the Court in many cases involving the construction of what at one time were called "treaties" and construed as such; but subsequently became contracts between the Tribes and the United States, and were so construed.

The Justice died very suddenly on Sunday morning, March 28, 1910. Only the evening before we had seen each other at a meeting of the Literary Club, where he expressed his views in regard to the relations of employers and employees, and cited some of his opinions dissenting from those of the majority of the Court, sustaining regulatory legislation in regard thereto.

In the famous New York Bakers' Case, which has previously been outlined, and in which the Supreme Court in 1905 held that the statute regulating the bakers' trade was unconstitutional, Justice Brewer joined with Justice Peckham—who wrote the opinion of the Court—in which he said:

"We think the limit of the police power has been reached and passed in this case."

To this Justice Harlan wrote the vigorous dissent in which Justices White and Day concurred. Justice Holmes wrote an individual dissent, which also has already been alluded to.

In a previous chapter, entitled "Memorial Tributes," Justice Brewer was included with Chief Justice Fuller, who died only a few months later. Therein the character and the judicial career of Justice Brewer are referred to at greater length.

JUSTICE HENRY B. BROWN (1890-1906)

THERE WERE frequent men's receptions given at 1535 Eye Street. In this respect we followed the example of my father who used to give men's receptions at Round Oak, the Yonkers family home, which were always most enjoyable affairs. My own family had no place in which such functions could be held until we came to Washington, and then we had them on numerous occasions.

The first one recorded in our Guest Book was given in honor of Justice Henry B. Brown of Michigan on his seventieth birthday, March 21, 1906. Several hundred invitations were issued and more than two hundred persons attended, and all seemed to enjoy themselves. As the names of many of the persons who attended that reception are of historic interest, several pages of the Guest Book with their signatures are reproduced on pages 191-192-193-194.

There was no collation but on various tables in the library, there were four punch bowls. Two contained punch made with champagne—an American brand, but a very good one, furnished by Demonet—cooled with iced fruit bricks. The other two bowls contained a non-alcoholic punch, subsequently named "Bryan Punch," which consisted of white grape juice and ginger ale, similarly cooled. On several tables were sandwiches, fried potatoes, cakes, etc.; cigars and cigarettes also were available.

The guests at this and our later receptions came for the sake of good fellowship, for they knew that while there would be no elaborate collation, there would be ample opportunity to converse with the other guests and have a pleasant evening. Mrs. Butler always had some of her lady friends help receive the guests in the front parlors and then escort them back to the library where the men congregated talking and partaking of the liquid and dry refreshments.

March 2, 1906

[signatures]

Charles W. Fairbanks

Melville W. Fuller

John M. Harlan

David J. Brewer

Henry B. Brown.

Joseph McKenna

E. D. White

Oliver Wendell Holmes

William R. Day

Seth Shepard

[Riley]

Job Barnard

Edward E. Hale

F. Fremont Smith.

Stanton J. Peelle

**GUESTS AT THE RECEPTION FOR JUSTICE BROWN,
MARCH 21, 1906**

191

[signatures]

Wm L. Chambers

J. P. Wood

Frank Sewall

O. H. Tittmann

Henry Wells

Bernard M. Newburg

Charles F. Wilson

William Henry Dennis

Alexander Porter Morse

Charles H. Duell

Wm A. Maury

Chas. B. Beall.

James Rudolph Garfield

J. A. Van Orsdel.

F. De Courcy Faust

Hamton C. Peelle.

John Ridout

Wendell Phillips Stafford

W B Lamar

Nathl Wilson.

GUESTS AT THE RECEPTION FOR JUSTICE BROWN,
MARCH 21, 1906

192

CHARLES HENRY BUTLER
1938

THE COVER OF THE PROGRAM OF THE SESQUICENTENNIAL
CELEBRATION

[Handwritten signatures of reception guests]

GUESTS AT THE RECEPTION FOR JUSTICE BROWN,
MARCH 21, 1906

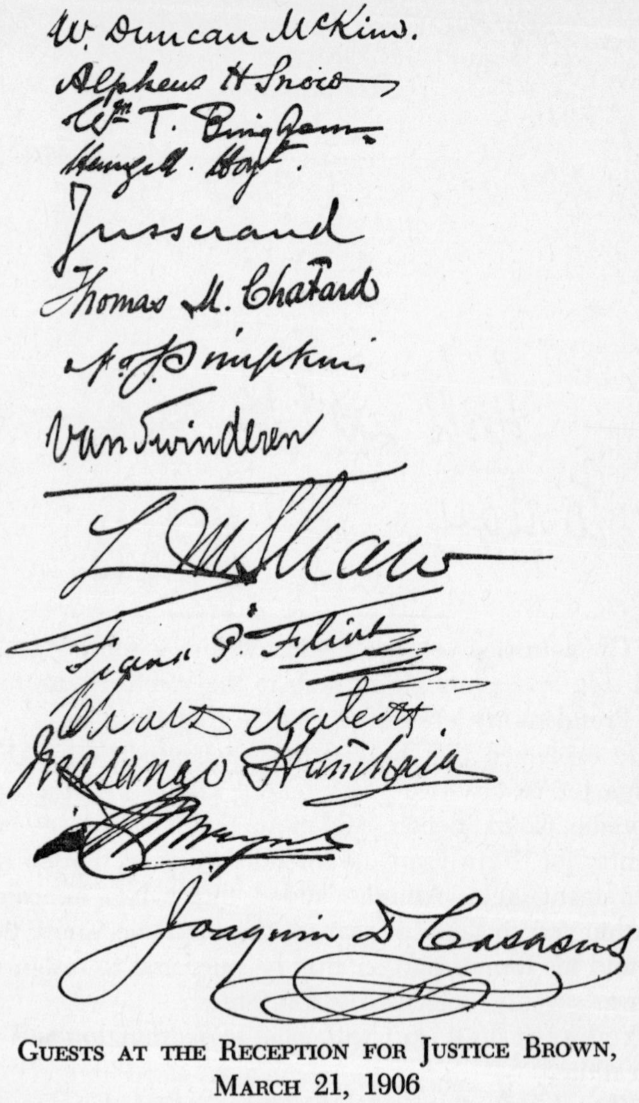

[signatures]

W. Duncan McKim.

Alpheus H. Snow

Wm T. Bingham

Hengell Hoyt.

Jusserand

Thomas M. Chatard

A. J. Simpkins

Van Swindleren

[illegible signature]

[illegible signature]

[illegible signature]

Masanao Hanihara

[illegible signature]

Joaquin D. Casasus

GUESTS AT THE RECEPTION FOR JUSTICE BROWN,
MARCH 21, 1906

On this occasion when all the guests except Justice and
Mrs. Brown had left, and we were sitting in the dining room,
enjoying a few minutes' conversation with them over a glass
of punch and a sandwich, Justice Brown said:

"Now I will tell you something. I have not told it to

194

Supreme Court of the United States.

Memorandum.

.... *1904*

*will walk up
to-day*   *HBB.*

the Chief Justice yet, but I will tell him tomorrow morning as I stop to see him on my way to the White House to give the President my letter of retirement from the Court."

He explained that he had been a United States District Judge for twenty-two years before taking his seat on the Supreme Court Bench, and now that he had served his country for thirty years, he intended to avail himself of the Retirement Act. Also he added that when he came to Washington to take his seat on the Supreme Court Bench, he told his former partner that he purposed to resign when he was seventy, and his friend returned:

"You won't do it, so I will come to Washington and make you retire."

When Justice Brown reached the Capitol the next morning, his old friend and partner met him with the salutation that he had come to pull him off the Bench.

"You can't do it," said Justice Brown, "because I have retired already."

His retirement took effect at the end of that term and

Saunders, S.B.
Mch. 31.

Dear Mr. Butler

We are booked to return home on the 8th and, if no accident occurs and the doctor does not interpose a veto, I shall hope to have the pleasure of being present at the reception to Mr. Justice Peckham at the House of the Champion Entertainer of Washington.

Loyally yours
H.B. Brown.

President Theodore Roosevelt appointed William H. Moody to succeed him.

Justice Rufus W. Peckham (1895-1909)

Justice Peckham of New York, who served from 1895 until 1909, was another of the Justices who was opposed to "sumptuary" legislation, as police regulation is called by many. He was generally arrayed with those who declared State Statutes governing relations between employers and employees unconstitutional because violative of the Fourteenth Amendment.

My friend, Edgar M. Cullen, at that time Chief Judge of the Court of Appeals, came to Washington frequently to visit his sisters who lived there, and more than once dined with us at our Eye Street home. On one occasion

196

when the dinner was given especially in honor of Chief Judge Cullen, Justice Peckham, who had served on the Court of Appeals with him, was unable to accept my invitation, but expressed the hope that Chief Judge Cullen would surely see him before leaving Washington.

Accordingly the next day Chief Judge Cullen rode up to the Capitol with me and sat with me inside the Bar. Justice Peckham sent for us to come behind the screen and there we had a very pleasant conversation. This turned immediately, as between the Justice and the Chief Judge, who were thoroughly in accord on the subject, on the iniquity of police legislation then being enacted by the States, some of which had been sustained and some overthrown by the Courts. They dwelt particularly on the Workmen's Compensation Acts, which many of the States were enacting at that time. Chief Judge Cullen had recently written an opinion in the Court of Appeals, Justice Peckham had written one in the Supreme Court; and each opinion upset one of those statutes.

"Ed," said Justice Peckham, "we must stand together now."

Then he expressed himself as greatly in fear of what has since happened. He mentioned no particular Justice, but it was evident to me that he was afraid of Justices Harlan and Holmes, and regarded them, as far as police statutes were concerned, as the dangerous elements in the Court.

Justice Peckham died October 24, 1909, and the United States Supreme Court attended his funeral in a body at Altamont just outside Albany.

Justice George Shiras, Jr. (1892-1903)

George Shiras, Jr., of Pennsylvania, who served from 1892 to 1903, was appointed to the Supreme Court of the United States by President Harrison when he was 60 years old.

Under the then controlling act a justice became eligible for retirement at any time after having served ten years and having attained at least seventy years of age. He declared that he intended to avail himself of the privilege as soon as he should become eligible.

He did not do so, however, until February 1903, when Justice William R. Day of Ohio was appointed by President Theodore Roosevelt. It was currently believed that in making this appointment President Roosevelt was carrying out the intention of his predecessor, President McKinley, for whom Mr. Day had been Secretary of State after the retirement of John Sherman.

Justice Shiras was a great fisherman. During the summer he would try his luck at a camp on Lake Michigan and in the winter he would transfer his fishing activities to Florida. On January 26, 1922, his ninetieth birthday was, as I knew, very appropriately celebrated by an assemblage of his family at Ormond Beach, Florida, and through me the Court also knew of the event.

That evening it was my good fortune to attend a dinner at which Chief Justice Taft was the guest of honor. In reply to my inquiry whether my message about Justice Shiras' birthday had been received, the Chief Justice answered:

"Yes, indeed, and all the Justices united in sending him a congratulatory telegram."

Then Chief Justice Taft began to chuckle as he frequently did when he had something amusing in the back of his mind. In answer to my question:

"What's the joke, Chief?" Mr. Taft told me in his dry humorous way how one of the younger Justices—not entitled to retire—had spoken of the luck of Shiras, who was able to fish all summer in Michigan, and all winter in Florida, and not have a thing on his mind except to draw his pay—"while we fellows have to work all day and all night to get ours."

"Yes," one of the older Justices observed, who could retire

198

whenever he wished, "but every time Shiras has been in Washington since he retired, he has told me that he regretted his retirement each day of his life."

JUSTICE JOSEPH McKENNA (1898-1925)

JUSTICE JOSEPH McKENNA, of California, served on the Bench of the Supreme Court of the United States from 1898 until 1925. Occasionally he talked with me about the difficulty he experienced in expressing his ideas and more than once referred to the same difficulty that has constantly confronted me in writing this little book, namely, the proper use of the third person singular. To whom does that last used "he," "him," or "his" refer? Some day a rhetorician or a grammarian may suggest the rule that will be universally adopted so that both writer and reader can visualize the personality meant by that ubiquitous and equivocal pronoun.

During the latter part of the Theodore Roosevelt Administration the McKennas occupied a rather small residence on Rhode Island Avenue. Here the marriage of one of the Justice's daughters took place. Outside the family and members and officers of the Supreme Court, the guests included only the President and his Cabinet and a few intimate friends.

As nearly everyone attending the function officially outranked me, my place was very near the front door lobby, where all the male guests had deposited their respective articles of headgear. At the conclusion of a very delightful event, as the guests were going away, a familiar voice exclaimed:

"Has anybody seen my hat?"

To this my reply was: "Mr. President, was it a new hat?"

The intention was to recall the famous incident when Abraham Lincoln, as a Congressman, attending a White House reception, was told on his objecting to accept a battered old headpiece from the hat room attendant, instead of the new silk hat he had purchased for the occasion, that:

"The second best hats were gone an hour ago."

President Roosevelt's assurance that his was not even a "second best hat," emboldened me to ask him whether a disreputable hat, but which did have the letters "T. R." punched in its band, might be his.

After examining the hat the President said:

"Yes, that is my hat—I recognize it." Turning to Attorney General Knox, he added: "And Knox, if I recognize this hat as mine, that makes it a fact, does it not?"

To this the Attorney General facetiously replied that it certainly did, especially as nobody else seemed to be claiming that particular hat. All this was very entertaining to those listening to the conversation because, just at the time, the most discussed governmental problem was the effect of the Presidential recognition of the newly formed Republic of Panama and the pending Panama Canal negotiations.

Shortly after my retirement, when meeting Chief Justice White and Justice McKenna, as they were walking homeward together along Connecticut Avenue, one of them asked me how it felt not to be any longer with the Court.

"In many respects," was my reply, "it's not so good, but there are some advantages."

"What, for instance?" asked Justice McKenna.

"Well," was my response, "the dissenting opinion can now be agreed with *out loud*, which could not be done before."

They both laughed, for they knew full well that everybody connected with the Court must be loyal to the "opinion of the Court." This eliminates more or less any audibly expressed agreement with the dissenting opinion, even though it may be surreptitiously agreed with.

not find it compatible to be associated with that firm at the same time. When Woodrow Wilson was elected Mr. Mc-Reynolds was practising law independently in New York.

Shortly after the Wilson Cabinet got into working order, Secretary of State Bryan invited me to call on him and Mrs. Bryan at the apartment they occupied in the New Willard. On my arrival they asked me to use my influence with the Attorney General—who was, they understood, "a very warm friend of mine,"—to procure the appointment of a young Floridian in whom they were interested. At one time this young Floridian had been my secretary, and they wanted to see him selected as the United States Attorney for the Southern District of Florida. They said he was highly endorsed by Governor Jennings, a cousin of William Jennings Bryan.

"But why ask me?" was my question. "You are Secretary of State, and why does not your influence with your fellow Cabinet member, Mr. McReynolds, far exceed mine?"

"Well," answered Secretary Bryan, "my influence in that direction does not seem to amount to much."

Not long thereafter I had an interview with the Attorney General and expressed my hope that the appointment would be made. My report to Secretary of State Bryan, as the result of that interview, was that the appointment was doubtful.

It happened that at a men's luncheon a few weeks later, the seats of the Secretary of State, of the Attorney General and of myself were near enough to make mutual conversation possible. Said the Secretary to me:

"Butler, why don't you ask the Attorney General how our friend's nomination is getting on?"

The question was passed by me to McReynolds, who replied:

"Butler, do you mean that fellow down there who's a friend of the Governor of Florida?"

"Yes, Mr. Attorney General, how about it?"

"Oh, that's getting on fine."

"What does that mean?"

"It means," responded the Attorney General, "that we've got him indicted with some other fellows on a land grant fraud—that's how it's getting on."

This was discouraging. In justice to my young Florida friend it must be added that he was entirely exonerated from the charges laid against him and the indictment was withdrawn. He was the victim of a political row between two factions. The one to which he did not belong was in the ascendant at the time, and it had been working against him on the basis that "all is fair in love, war and politics." However, he did get a State appointment, which he filled very well. He married a rich woman and lived happily— but not forever after, as he died only a short time after the events here recited.

This was one of the few instances which proved the advisability of my otherwise invariable rule for the last forty years not to endorse people—especially friends—for public office.

Another of these rare instances happened when a friend worried me into a promise to speak a good word to the Attorney General for him in regard to a judicial post he was seeking. Seeing the Attorney General walking a little ahead of me one day, it seemed as good an opportunity as any to redeem my promise. After catching up with Mr. McReynolds, and exchanging greetings, my remarks continued to the effect that Mr. Soandso, as Mr. McReynolds doubtless knew, was an aspirant for the vacant judgeship and had asked me to say a good word for him.

A day or so later when my friend happened to meet me, and was told of this meeting, he inquired anxiously:

"What did the Attorney General say?"

He was rather shattered by my answer:

"The Attorney General looked at me and said: 'Mr. Butler, do you know we are having a very late spring this year?'"

204

[handwritten letter]

The RochaomBeau
Dec. 29"

Many, many times I thank my friend Charles Henry Butler Esq. for a box of lovely apples which have gladdened the holiday time for me.

He is certainly a true man — a generous soul and may he live many, many years in peace and contentment.'

Faithfully
J. C. McReynolds

Chas Henry Butler Esq

The Attorney General and I had come to a convenient parting of the ways just then; and that ended my efforts to fill that particular vacant judicial chair.

Mr. McReynolds remained Attorney General until President Wilson appointed him Justice of the Supreme Court of the United States in 1914 to succeed Justice Lurton.

JUSTICE EDWARD T. SANFORD (1923-1930)

JUSTICE EDWARD T. SANFORD of Tennessee served on the Supreme Court of the United States from 1923 to 1930. Our acquaintance with the Justice and Mrs. Sanford began when he came to Washington as Assistant Attorney General in 1907 and on more than one occasion they were welcome guests at our Eye Street entertainments. In 1908 he was appointed District Judge for the Eastern District of Tennessee and moved back to Nashville. In 1923 President Harding selected him to fill the vacancy on the Supreme Court Bench caused by the retirement of Associate Justice Day; and we were glad indeed to have the Sanfords return to Washington.

They joined the American Bar Association pilgrimage abroad in 1924, crossed with us on the *Berengaria*, and were co-guests with us at many of the entertainments given by our British hosts during our stay in London. Justice Sanford was one of the American speakers at the Lord Mayor's Guildhall banquet to which, owing to the limited accommodations, only a small fraction of the Americans could be invited; but it was my good fortune to be included among the American guests.

Justice Sanford had told me on shipboard that he had been informed by radio he was to be one of the two Americans to speak at the Lord Mayor's banquet; and he asked my advice as to how long he should talk, at the same time suggesting he should not exceed half an hour.

"Half an hour!" was my reply, "from my information about the Lord Mayor's banquet, few speakers take more than ten, and none more than fifteen minutes."

My information was correct, as demonstrated by the fact that no one at the banquet exceeded those time limits except Justice Sanford. He made a very good speech, but went beyond his fifteen minutes of allotted time by nearly ten minutes, somewhat upsetting the schedule.

It was my conversation on the *Berengaria* that inspired the following lines in a little skit written for the Ship's Concert, in which I referred to members of the Bar Association, who were busy at the writing desks in the lounge preparing the *impromptu* remarks they expected to deliver at the various functions to be given on our arrival in London:

"Let us hope they all remember, if not, this hint I'll drop,
Good after-dinner speaking is knowing when to stop."

However, no one begrudged Justice Sanford the extra time he took because what he said was well worth hearing.

While the Sanfords were living in Nashville they made frequent visits to Washington. On one of these visits they dined at Eye Street, when Wu Ting Fang, then Chinese Minister to the United States, was present.

The Chinese Minister and Mrs. Sanford became actively engaged in a discussion of what is generally known as "vegetarianism," but which Wu Ting Fang called "sandadarianism," and its effect on longevity. Wu Ting Fang reaffirmed what he had been quoted by the press as saying, namely, that if properly adhered to, sandadarian diets would result in the followers of them living two hundred years.

Justice Sanford's death was even more sudden than that of Justice Brewer. Starting from his apartment for the usual Saturday Conference of the Court one Saturday in March 1930, he stopped at his dentist's. While in the dentist chair, and during the examination of a tooth that had been troubling him, he suddenly expired.

His colleagues were stunned when the Clerk, who had been instructed to ascertain the cause of the delay of Justice Sanford, announced that the Member of the Court for whom they were waiting, would not be late in arriving at the conference, but would never be present at another session of the Court.

Mrs. Sanford survived him until the summer of 1939 and was among the many—unfortunately far too many—friends of the author who have died during the preparation of this volume for publication.

CHAPTER XVII

THE SUPREME COURT AS IT WAS, IS NOW, AND EVER SHALL BE

WHILE THIS volume was being prepared for publication, the Supreme Court of the United States, its decisions and its personnel, have been more constantly in the public eye, and to a greater extent under public discussion, than at any other period within my own experience, even when special events have occurred to attract attention to them.

In his address at the memorial meeting for Chief Justice Waite in 1888, my father, as quoted elsewhere, said that the country was at that time more conscious of the Supreme Court than he had ever known it to be before. After President Franklin Delano Roosevelt's message to Congress in February 1937, Alice Roosevelt Longworth, in one of her daily [press] items said: "The country was never so Supreme Court conscious as it is today."

Within a few months, at the greatest legal gathering of the year, one prominent member of the Bar characterized the action of the Supreme Court as tending toward instability rather than stability; yet another prominent member extolled the Court for the very reasons which had been the basis of the criticism of the orator preceding him.

But the discussion regarding the Court has not been confined to members of the Bar or to those in public life. It has extended to the man in the street and to the business world, as the following personal incident demonstrates.

Shortly after President Franklin Roosevelt's famous "horse and buggy" remarks about the Supreme Court, two men,

208

THE SUPREME COURT OF THE UNITED STATES
1940

Seated, left to right: Associate Justice Owen J. Roberts; Associate Justice James Clark McReynolds; Chief Justice Charles Evans Hughes; Associate Justice Harlan Fiske Stone; Associate Justice Hugo L. Black.

Standing, left to right: Associate Justice William O. Douglas; Associate Justice Stanley F. Reed; Associate Justice Felix Frankfurter; Associate Justice Frank Murphy.

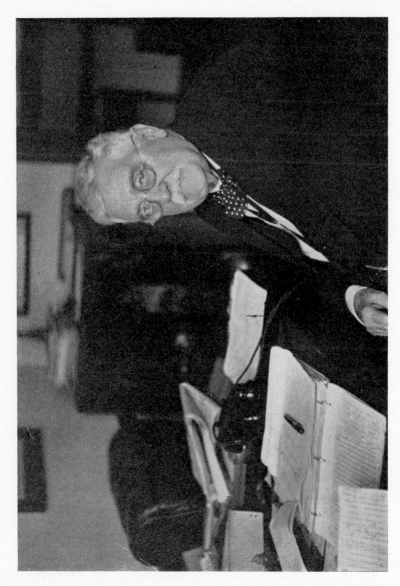

CHARLES HENRY BUTLER
Working on the Manuscript of this Book

talking excitedly to each other, entered a Washington restaurant at lunch time, and sat directly opposite me. Continuing their conversation, one of them said:

"And so I shall never vote for him again."

"But," the other returned, "you voted for him both times before this."

"Yes," was the retort, "but that was before he had said anything about the Supreme Court. I'm not a lawyer, but I believe in the Supreme Court."

"Well," his friend warned, "you have a lot of friends who will want you to vote for him."

But the other stood by his guns, saying:

"I don't care who asks me to vote for him, I won't do it after what he said about the Supreme Court. Of course, if Jesus Christ should come down and ask me to vote for him, I'd do it—but I wouldn't do it for St. Peter and I wouldn't do it for St. Paul."

Then they ordered lunch and, having finished my own, the opportunity was given me, as I departed, to say:

"You're all right. I *am* a lawyer and am also all for the Supreme Court."

The sentiment thus strongly expressed is, in my opinion, that of the great majority of American citizens, who, whether they do or do not fully understand all the intricacies of our Federal system of government, do know that there *is* a Supreme Court of the United States, which can be relied upon to protect the rights of the American people.

There is undoubtedly a spirit of unrest in the minds of part of our population regarding the Court, its decisions and its personnel. Undoubtedly also there are some who think that neither recent decisions nor lately appointed judges have strengthened it so far as it is the bulwark of the personal liberties and the protection of the life and the property of the people of the United States. These views are not shared by me, however, nor has my respect for, nor my faith

209

in, the Supreme Court been shattered or even shaken. As my oft-quoted father said in one of his addresses:

"It is the Supreme Court as a whole which is the conservator and interpreter of our constitutional rights, and it is not so much its highest honor to have been, or to be presided over, or to include, men of unmatched abilities, if indeed that could be claimed, but that as a Court it has been steadily true to the trust and equal to the trust with which the people have invested it; that it has kept pace with the growing needs of the country, and has itself grown in wisdom with the nation's growth in wealth and power."

The present anxiety and criticism is not new in the annals of American history. One hundred years ago, after the death of Chief Justice Marshall, when President Jackson appointed Roger B. Taney as Chief Justice, similar gloomy forebodings were expressed by many of our citizens as to the fate of the high tribunal and the effect of that appointment on its prestige. In his "History of the Supreme Court" Charles Warren relates that Daniel Webster wrote to a friend:

"Judge Story thinks the Supreme Court is *gone*, and I think so too."

Chancellor Kent, as quoted by Chief Justice Hughes in one of his lectures, referred to the Court as a "melancholy mess." Newspaper editorials in more than one section of the country expressed like views. But the Court and its great prestige, and the faith of the people in its integrity, have survived, and still do and in my opinion they will continue not only to survive, but to increase in strength as the years go by.

The Constitution gives to the President of the United States the right, subject to confirmation by the Senate, of making appointments to the Supreme, as well as to all other Courts of the United States. The President is the choice of the people at large, as the Senators are the choice of the people of the States they represent.

In selecting nominees to fill Federal offices all Presidents have chosen and doubtless will continue to choose men believed to be in sympathy with their policies. This applies to appointments to the Bench as well as for other appointive posts. President Jackson followed this practice when he appointed Mr. Taney as Chief Justice. President Taft appointed five members of the Court, besides promoting Justice White to the Chief Justiceship. All these appointees were sympathetic to President Taft's own conservative legal mind.

President Theodore Roosevelt appointed Justice Oliver Wendell Holmes, who was regarded as broadminded, but not radical; and he also appointed Justice Day and Justice Moody, one of whom had served in the Cabinet of President McKinley and the other in his own.

President Wilson appointed Justice McReynolds, who was a member of his Cabinet; and also Justice Brandeis and Justice Clarke, who were known to be Mr. Wilson's ardent supporters. President Harding appointed ex-President Taft to be Chief Justice. President Coolidge appointed Justice Sutherland and Justice Butler and also Justice Stone, who, after a few years on the Bench, drifted far apart from his fellow appointees of Mr. Coolidge. President Hoover not only appointed Chief Justice Hughes, but also Justice Roberts and Justice Cardozo. The latter was of the opposing political party, but it was realized that he would be, as he certainly was, acceptable to the confirming power and to the people at large.

President Franklin Delano Roosevelt appointed five of the Justices now sitting on the Bench. All these appointees probably share Mr. Roosevelt's views, which indubitably are not shared by many people in this country; but these appointees are men of ability and strength of mind and character. The selection of Justice Black was criticized by many who acclaimed the appointment of Justice Reed; yet these two Justices have seen eye to eye on many occasions. Justice Frankfurter, Justice Douglas and Justice Murphy are, in President Franklin Delano Roosevelt's opinion, believers in his policies, otherwise he would not have chosen them.*

Whether any of these appointees, or other members of the Court, may be styled liberal, reactionary, radical or conservative, inclined to be firm for States' Rights or for Federal Sovereignty, the decisions of the Court must necessarily be determined by its majority at the time when rendered.

The views of the majority have changed from time to time as the nation has elected the appointing power to fill vacancies on the Bench. The Supreme Court, nevertheless, will continue to function as a unit. Although it may—because of the change in popular opinion as reflected in its personnel—have shocked at times the sensibilities of some who are always shocked by change, it will still be the palladium of our liberties and will justify the inscription emblazoned on the pediment of the building in which it has been established.

This change in personnel has often resulted in the overruling of earlier decisions construing provisions of the Constitution. But the novel constructions placed on such provisions have not had the disastrous results predicted. No recent decision that reversed a prior ruling of the Court has resulted in any greater change in our judicial history than that rendered in 1851 when the Court handed down its opinion in the *Genesee Chief* † and overruled its previous decisions. Admiralty jurisdiction of the Federal Courts, under the Constitution, had been limited to cases arising within the ebb and flow of the tide, as was the rule in England, and this overruling made navigability, instead of tide, the test of jurisdiction. Thus all the great navigable waters of the United States were brought under Federal Judicial control.

That decision was rendered by a divided Court. The

* These comments were written in 1940. Since then President Roosevelt has appointed two more Justices, Mr. Justice Jackson and Mr. Justice Byrnes and he elevated Associate Justice Stone to the office of Chief Justice. Ed.

† (12 Howard 443.)

minority clung to the rule announced by no less an authority on constitutional construction than Chief Justice Marshall; yet it showed that the Court had kept pace with the growing needs of the country. With regard to this epochal decision, Charles O'Conor, one of the ablest members of the American Bar, said in an argument in the New York Court of Appeals:

"That Admiralty jurisdiction could exist without tide-water or salt-water was an idea too novel for even the great mind of Chief Justice Marshall, but at last judicial wisdom, sharpened and impelled by strong necessity, cast aside these immaterial incidents and, looking at the substance of the thing, found in the Constitution a government for our great rivers and inland seas."

In quoting Mr. O'Conor my father added to this statement:

"It was reserved for the Court in which Chief Justice Taney presided to announce the final establishment of this enlarged grant of power which Marshall and Story had denied, and for the Court over which Chief Justice Waite has just ceased to preside, to give to it even wider scope in aid of the commercial interests of the nation."

The overruling of the first Legal Tender Case by the second case of that name may have caused much worriment to some minds; yet the right of the Government of the United States to issue money to enable it to function was necessary for its existence. Many other instances of the overruling of decisions are referred to in Mr. Hughes' second lecture on the Supreme Court which was delivered at Columbia University.

Later decisions, apparently further expanding the definition of interstate commerce and to the same extent overruling former limitations thereof, have simply restated the definition of what, in my opinion, was contemplated originally by the interstate commerce clause of the Constitution as that class of commerce has developed with the development of the country.

It is not at all impossible that sooner or later the great

213

mercantile and industrial organizations that fought the extension of Interstate Commerce in the Jones & Laughlin,* and other similar cases, will be claiming protection under Federal law in preference, or even in opposition, to like laws enacted by the States. To a great extent that has happened in situations concerning transportation matters under the control of the Interstate Commerce Commission. Yet the constitutionality of the Act instituting the commission and giving it the powers it possesses, was bitterly attacked when it first became a law.

My own feelings cannot be expressed in regard to the Supreme Court of the United States, nor can this volume be brought to an end, more fittingly than by quoting the closing words of my father's address at the Judiciary Centennial in New York City fifty years ago:

"On this centenary of its organization; in the city where its earliest jurisdiction was exercised; in the presence of the Chief Executive, of the heads of our National Legislature, of our highest State Courts and officers, of citizens representing all the activities of the country, and in the face of the world, we make profert of this high tribunal as a proof of the stability and abiding strength of our free constitutional government. As members of the Bar, and as citizens of this State and of the United States, we bring to it and bespeak for it the homage of national gratitude and of universal respect, not so much because it has added illustrious names to the roll of the world's great jurists and magistrates, or even because it has so well upheld, in its own sphere, the honor and dignity of the nation, as because through all these hundred years of time it has, with strict fidelity, without fear and without favor, with clean hands and with a pure purpose, served the people in the wise and patient execution of its high trust to maintain inviolate the absolute supremacy of Justice."

* (301 U.S. 1.)

214

INDEX

A

Admiralty law, 4-42

Admission to the Supreme Court bar, 117-123

Alaska, Territory of, case of constitutionality of law, 92-93

Alaska Boundary Commission case, 72-73

Albany Regency, 30-31

Alexander, DeAlva S., "Political History of the State of New York," 31

Allen, Benjamin F., 11

Allen, William Henry, 7

Allen, William Howard, 6-7, 34

Alverstone, Lord, 72, 73

America (yacht), and the Queen's Cup, 56

American Bar Association, visit to London (1924), 206-207

Announcements of decisions, 94-97

Anti-trust case, Standard Oil, 169

Apples from Montsweag Farm, 102-103, 155-157, 158-159, 205

Appointing power, decision on, 24-25

Appointments, Presidential, 211-212

Arguing at the Supreme Court bar, 114-116

Argument, time for, 86-87

Arguments, written vs. oral, 94

Arnoux, William H., 140

B

Bakers' Case, 170-172, 189

Bancroft, George, 27

Banks Law Publishing Co., 71

Barbour, Philip P., 18, 150

Beardsley, Charles A., 150

Beardsley, Samuel, 33

Beck, James M., 120-121

Benedict, Robert D., 50, 60

Benedict Collar Button Case, 89

Benton, Thomas H., 17

Bethune, Dr. George W., 36

Bidwell, Maxwell S., 35

Black, Hugo L., 211

Blackstone vs. *Miller*, 77-79

Blatchford, Samuel A., 144, 160-161; death of, 137

Bloom, Sol, 150

Boundary dispute, New York and New Jersey, 5-6

Bradley, Joseph P., 48, 90-91

Brandeis, Louis D., 182, 211

Brewer, David Josiah, 65, 75, 86, 90, 99, 133, 166-167, 188-190; Memorial Note, 133-136; death of, 134, 189; tribute by Chief Justice Fuller, 136-137

Bronson, Greene C., 33

Brown, Charles F., 120

Brown, Henry B., 65, 71, 92, 184, 190-196; death of, 137; facsimile of letter from, 196

Bryan, William Jennings, 203

Bryce, James, 101, 104, 105

Buchanan, James, 161

Burr, Aaron, 9

Butler, Benjamin F., 1-36; "Notes of the Reporter," 10; tribute of William Allen Butler, 33-34

Butler, Mrs. Benjamin Franklin, 22-23

215

DATE DUE